If you're eager to thrive in the changing workplace, *In Control at 50+* is a must-read. Workplace futurist Kerry Hannon provides a blueprint for setting audacious goals, shaping and growing your network, and getting the job you desire—now and in the future.

—**DORIE CLARK,** *Wall Street Journal* bestselling
author of *The Long Game* and Executive Education
faculty at Duke University Fuqua School of Business

Kerry Hannon's *In Control at 50+: How to Succeed in the New World of Work* is an essential guide with grounded details for landing a job or making a life transition. Hannon offers new models and resources with a step-by-step plan for tackling the complexities of the postpandemic work life. Takeaways are based on a commonsense strategy to reinvent the average person's own experience and help them achieve success. This book has everything you need.

—**CINDY HOUNSELL,** President of Women's Institute
for a Secure Retirement (WISER)

Kerry Hannon steers you through the rapidly changing world of work, whether you're launching a business, making a career transition, or seeking a new job. Not only does she lead you forward on a new path with moxie and confidence, she also stresses that lifelong education is *the* magic ingredient that will enhance your career, build resilience, and allow you to be open to discover joy and meaning in what you do and the lives you touch.

—**CHIP CONLEY,** *New York Times* bestselling
author of *Emotional Equations* and
Founder of the Modern Elder Academy

No one explains the challenges facing midcareer workers better than Kerry Hannon. Her new book is an insightful look at how the Covid-19 pandemic has shaped today's job market for older workers and provides a road map to opportunities to ensure that they are not left behind as we move forward. This book is a must-read for all interested in creating an inclusive labor market that doesn't ignore the needs and wants of a vital and vibrant segment of that market—the older worker.

—RAMONA SCHINDELHEIM, Editor in Chief of WorkingNation

This is the book to read for anyone over 50, or nearing that age, who plans to work full-time or part-time. With timely advice from Hannon and a bevy of sharp experts, there's loads of practical information on finding jobs, making yourself more employable, and finding fulfillment. Worth every penny.

—RICHARD EISENBERG, former Managing Editor of Next Avenue and Executive Editor of *Money* magazine

Midcareer workers are under-tapped talent. They often face age bias when looking for employment, particularly when they are seeking to switch careers. At a time in which many industries are experiencing labor shortages, and people are living and working longer, an intergenerational workforce is more important than ever. Kerry Hannon offers valuable insights for job seekers age 50+ to navigate the labor market landscape.

—MONA MOURSHED, founding CEO of Generation

Kerry Hannon's prescient understanding of the labor market allows her to deliver a pragmatic, yet positive, assessment for older workers. She offers actionable steps that all individuals can take today to build relevancy and respect in the Super Age workforce.

—BRADLEY SCHURMAN, demographic futurist and author of *The Super Age*

Many aspects of aging aren't under our control, but one very important aspect is: our attitude. How do we handle our inner ageist, who whispers, "Am I too old to learn new skills?" "Do I have the energy?" "Will someone want to hire me?" In her expert and engaging guide to succeeding in the twenty-first-century workplace, Kerry Hannon explains how to arrive at "no," "yes," and "yes!"

—**ASHTON APPLEWHITE,** author of *This Chair Rocks*

In Control at 50+ is the IT guide for those who seek to demystify the daunting changes of age and see past to new opportunity. Empathetically written and intellectually challenging, this book empowers readers seeking to reimagine themselves and the path they see ahead for the better.

—**SANYIN SIANG,** professor at Duke University, CEO coach, and author of *The Launch Book*

As the world's population is aging faster than ever before, Kerry's book brings together deep research and insights on how the future of work is not only changing for those 50+ but can be advantageous in an economy that values knowledge and remote work.

—**NEIL DSOUZA,** Cofounder and CEO of GetSetUp

IN CONTROL AT 50+

How to Succeed in the New World of Work

KERRY HANNON

Mc
Graw
Hill

NEW YORK   CHICAGO   SAN FRANCISCO   ATHENS   LONDON
MADRID   MEXICO CITY   MILAN   NEW DELHI
SINGAPORE   SYDNEY   TORONTO

1 2 3 4 5 6 7 8 9   LCR   27 26 25 24 23 22

ISBN 978-1-264-26659-3
MHID   1-264-26659-6

e-ISBN 978-1-264-26660-9
e-MHID   1-264-26660-X

Library of Congress Cataloging-in-Publication Data

Names: Hannon, Kerry, author.
Title: In control at 50+ : how to succeed in the new world of work / Kerry
  Hannon.
Other titles: In control at fifty plus
Description: 1 Edition. | New York : McGraw Hill, [2022] | Includes
  bibliographical references and index.
Identifiers: LCCN 2021057768 (print) | LCCN 2021057769 (ebook) | ISBN
  9781264266593 (hardback) | ISBN 9781264266609 (ebook)
Subjects: LCSH: Job hunting—United States. | Older
  people—Employment—United States. | Middle-aged
  persons—Employment—United States.
Classification: LCC HF5382.75.U6 H3632 2022 (print) | LCC HF5382.75.U6
  (ebook) | DDC 331.702084/60973—dc23/eng/20220121
LC record available at https://lccn.loc.gov/2021057768
LC ebook record available at https://lccn.loc.gov/2021057769

For always believing in me and my dreams—
Marguerite "Mugs" Sullivan Hannon—
your grace, laughter, and love live on in my heart

Contents

Foreword

by **Catherine Collinson**
CEO and President of Transamerica Institute and
Transamerica Center for Retirement Studies

Looking back, it is hard to believe that the US unemployment rate was at a historic low at the beginning of 2020—and that by April, it had skyrocketed to heights unseen since the 1930s and the Great Depression. In addition to being a public health crisis, the Covid-19 pandemic wreaked havoc on businesses and disrupted longstanding employment trends. Some businesses successfully adjusted to the new environment, while others permanently shuttered.

Employment shocks can be daunting for everyone, but they can be especially challenging for older workers. Time and again, history has shown that it is more difficult for older workers to find meaningful employment, if any at all, amid societal headwinds of ageism. Many older job seekers become discouraged and retire before they are financially and emotionally ready to do so. It should not be this way. We need to rewrite this story's ending.

Change brings opportunity. The pandemic exposed weaknesses in our society, infrastructure, social safety nets, and daily lives. But it also affirmed what we value: family and friends, community, and our ability to enjoy life. The knowledge and experience gained from the pandemic will fuel innovation, new businesses, and better ways of doing work—and it will take people to transform these opportunities into reality.

Older workers, whom I prefer to call "experienced employees," bring wisdom, expertise, and problem-solving skills to a multigenerational workforce. Speaking as an experienced employee, I know that our ability to achieve success in the working world begins with a profound belief in the possibilities—a vote of confidence in ourselves— and relentless perseverance.

We have the potential to live longer than in any other period in history. This exciting gift invites us to reimagine our life journeys, including the amount of time we spend in the workforce relative to retirement. Many people have been thinking on these terms and expect to work beyond the traditional retirement age of 65. Today, two-thirds of workers aged 50+ at for-profit companies (66 percent) and almost four in five self-employed workers (79 percent) expect to retire after age 65 or do not plan to retire at all, according to findings from a survey conducted by the nonprofit Transamerica Center for Retirement Studies® in late 2020.[1] Moreover, fewer than one in five said their retirement plans had changed because of the pandemic.

It isn't all about the money either. When asked why they planned to work beyond age 65 or continue working in retirement, most cited both financial and healthy aging–related reasons, ranging from wanting or needing the income to enjoying what they do and having a sense of purpose. Yet, our survey findings uncovered a major disconnect. Many 50+ workers are not proactive about taking steps to help ensure they can work as long as they want and need. Specifically, among those employed by for-profit companies, only 62 percent are focused on staying healthy so they can continue working and just

44 percent are keeping their job skills up to date. Even fewer are networking and meeting new people (16 percent), taking classes to learn new skills (12 percent), scoping out the employment market and opportunities available (10 percent), attending virtual conferences and webinars (9 percent), or obtaining a new degree, certification, or professional designation (5 percent).

As experienced employees who are extending our working lives, we are blazing a new trail. We are challenging the status quo, redefining work and retirement, personifying the endless possibilities, and creating role models that future generations can follow. Yes, it is hard work, but success is increasingly within reach. Employers are beginning to recognize the value of experienced employees and are becoming more inclusive in their approaches to recruiting and retaining workers. A silver lining of the pandemic is that more employers are accommodating alternative work arrangements. Out of necessity, work went remote, with more flexible schedules—and employers discovered their employees were just as productive. This bodes well for the work-life balance of workers of all ages and, particularly, experienced employees who may have caregiving responsibilities, wish to reduce their work hours and transition into retirement, or just want the flexibility. And thanks to the proliferation of the digital marketplace and gig economy, many of the self-employment barriers have diminished or disappeared altogether. The available services for the self-employed include legal, finance, web development, marketing, and public relations, among many others. There is greater opportunity than ever before.

In my travels as a researcher, I am often approached by experienced employees who want to make a change in their lives or have been forced to do so. They are unhappy with their current situations, worried about their continued employment, or have lost their jobs. During our conversations, they share their self-doubt and ask: Will prospective employers even consider me? What are the options for someone my age? Where do I begin (deep sigh)?

In Control at 50+: How to Succeed in the New World of Work provides a road map for navigating the employment market and transitioning into retirement in today's environment. In this empowering how-to guide, Kerry Hannon masterfully illustrates how Covid-19 has changed the nature of work, provides a compelling vision of the future, and highlights opportunities and specific action steps for achieving success. Along the way, she reminds us of our value and shows how we can live with purpose and joy.

Acknowledgments

Thank you first and foremost to my McGraw Hill executive editor, Casey Ebro, and agent, Linda Konner at the Linda Konner Literary Agency. It's the strong vision of these two women that propelled this project amid the global pandemic. They recognized the future demand for a playbook to successfully guide workers 50+ in a profoundly changed job market.

To Kevin Commins, thanks for the skilled, smooth editing—and for the laughter. You are the bee's knees.

A huge round of applause to the following experts who shared their insights with me: Marci Alboher, Nancy Ancowitz, Barbara Brooks, Dorie Clarke, Alisa Cohn, Nancy Collamer, Catherine Collinson (special thanks for your spot-on Foreword), Chip Conley, Donna M. De Carolis, Neil Dsouza, Ken and Maddy Dychtwald, Kimberly A. Eddleston, Sharon Emek, Marc Freedman, Joseph Fuller, Mary Furlong, Cecelia Gerard, Cal J. Halvorsen, Guadalupe Hirt, Cindy Hounsell, Paul Irving, Elizabeth Isele, Richard Johnson, Susan P. Joyce, Bonnie Marcus, Mark Miller, Dorian Mintzer, Hannah Morgan, Mona Mourshed, Nathalie Molina Niño, Philip Pizzo, Gwenn Rosener, Dan Schawbel, Ramona Schindelheim, Thomas Schreier Jr., Bradley Schurman, Ofer Sharone, Sanyin Siang, Simon Sinek, Sara Sutton, John Tarnoff, Jeff Tidwell, Angela F. Williams, and Luke Yoquinto.

A special shout-out and deep appreciation to Chris Farrell, my colleague along this path, who has deeply reported this important seismic shift in our culture with his terrific books, *Purpose and a Paycheck* and *UnRetirement*.

To the many people who shared their work stories with me, including David Conti, Edith Cooper, Keith Cooper, Marjorie Dorr, Russ Eanes, Lisa K. Fitzpatrick, Gayle Jennings-O'Byrne, Carol Nash, Billy Spitzer, Dave Summers, Jordan Taylor, and Gayle Williams-Byers—thanks for opening the door into your journey for others to learn and be inspired.

A special nod to Beverly Jones, executive coach, savvy career strategist, author of *Find Your Happy at Work: 50 Ways to Get Unstuck, Move Past Boredom, and Discover Fulfillment* and *Think Like an Entrepreneur, Act Like a CEO*, and, I'm honored to say, dear friend and fellow dog walker.

Huge thanks to Richard Eisenberg, former managing editor of Next Avenue and former executive editor of *Money* magazine. Rich has been fine-tuning my work, keeping me curious, and pushing the conversation on work and jobs for people over 50 in meaningful ways for many years now. Much of the work I've done on this topic has been developed with Rich for Next Avenue.

To my *New York Times* editor, Jane Bornemeier, a deep appreciation for your support and encouragement and keen focus on telling the stories of second act entrepreneurs and creative approaches to work and retirement.

Angela Moore, my *MarketWatch* editor, your positive encouragement and insight on my work and retirement commentary has been such a breath of fresh air.

Janna Herron, I am thrilled to be a member of your dynamite team at Yahoo Finance. I look forward to exploring and revealing more insights about the future world of work together and making a positive impact on people's lives and future financial security.

The centering core and ballast of my work—family and friends.

Infinite thanks for all the love and support from my mom, Marguerite "Mugs" Sullivan Hannon, who passed way August 3, 2021, on the cusp of turning 92. She was my lifelong cheerleader and believed in me with all her heart. She made the world a more beautiful place.

Heartfelt appreciation to my go-to home team, the Bonney family: Paul, Pat, Christine, Mike, Caitlin, Shannon, Garrett Goon, Eileen Roach Bonney, Lindsay Corner Bonney, and Kodi; the Hannon family: Mike, Judy, Brendan (Max), Sean (Emily), Conor, Brian, and Charmaine; the Hersch family: Ginny, David, Corey, and Amy; and the Hackel family: Stu, Sue, Cassie, and Eric.

Especially for Jack, who wrestled to find meaningful work at 50+: I miss you, brother. I hope this book helps others who face similar obstacles find success.

And to my sidekick and dearest pal, Marcy Holquist, for sharing Icelandic chocolate and laughter and, importantly, for listening.

Deep gratitude to Amy Zettler and all my horse friends and, particularly, my ringside cheerleaders and therapists at Woodhall Farm in Aldie, Virginia, including Dale Crittenberger, Laura Schroff Scaletti, Lydia Davidson, and, most especially, Peter Foley, a true horseman, whose kindness and honesty I treasure more than any blue ribbon.

To my horse of a lifetime, blessed with a heart of gold and utmost patience, Caparino Z. To Elmore "Elly," my Labrador retriever puppy, who has shown me once again the importance of keeping our hearts open for new love to enter. Thanks, Jane Kelso!

Lastly, to my husband, Cliff Hackel, who encourages me to keep learning every day and striving to make a difference in the world.

The majority of material and the stories you will discover here are derived from my own research and reporting. Several, however, come from the many entrepreneurs, workers, and experts I've met through my career. Some of them initially shared their experience and journey with me for articles I have written or in the back-and-forth during one of my speaking engagements, podcasts, radio shows, or webinars. Others shared their experiences specifically for this book. Unless otherwise noted, all the stories and quotes in the book, including those from various experts, come from these interviews.

The New World of Work

Crush. Covid-19 ripped through the global workplace starting in 2020. It spawned job losses and shattered businesses. It triggered many older workers who lost jobs or were offered early retirement severance packages to leave the workforce—often earlier than planned.

It happened fast. It was breathtakingly brutal. And no one was prepared.

Older workers who lost their jobs due to the pandemic did so at a higher rate than their younger counterparts.

For small businesses it was shattering, particularly for those with older owners. At the peak of the first wave of the pandemic in the spring of 2020, more than 20 percent of small businesses closed shop, according to the Federal Reserve Bank of New York and AARP.[1] Business shutdowns were highest among owners age 45 and older, with one in four closing. Although the overall number of small businesses subsequently improved, the number of firms owned by people 45 and older were slower to bounce back.

One silver lining of the pandemic was that it allowed more people to work remotely. Once a coveted perk for workers, remote work became the norm for white-collar employees. The genie had jumped out of the bottle! Employers scrambled to make it work. Employees learned how to connect virtually, and they tried their best to balance work demands with their own set of personal responsibilities, which often included increased child- and eldercare duties.

I juggled caring for my 91-year-old mom with dementia after my siblings and I sprang her from her assisted care apartment when the building went into lockdown/isolation mode early in the pandemic. I hung by a thread at times, mentally and physically, trying to keep up with my work and doing everything I could for Mom.

Many workers, including me, are still grappling with the psychological impact of the pandemic on their working lives. In 2020, 7 out of 10 people experienced more stress and anxiety than any year previously, according to global research by Oracle and Workplace Intelligence. Four out of 10 people said they encountered increased pressure to meet performance standards and unmanageable workloads. And 41 percent had trouble drawing boundaries between working hours and personal home life.[2]

The good news was the economy rallied and the unemployment picture for older workers improved following the worst of the pandemic, according to the U.S. Bureau of Labor Statistics (BLS). Many older workers returned to the labor force as the economy rebounded and vaccines became widely available.[3]

A report by the researchers at the Center for Retirement Research at Boston College was in synch with previous findings of the pre-Covid trend of boomers working longer to set themselves up for better financial footing when they *do* retire. There was one exception— workers ages 70 and over saw a statistically significant increase in their likelihood of retirement during the pandemic.

Businesses are expected to increase pay an average of 3.9 percent in 2022, according to a Conference Board report. That's the fastest wage spurt since 2008. Job openings are at a record number, and it's likely that "severe labor shortages will continue through 2022," according to the findings. "During that time, overall wage growth is likely to remain well above four percent. Wages for new hires, and workers in blue-collar and manual services jobs will grow faster than average."[4]

And a total of 26 states and Washington, DC, have announced raises in minimum wage in 2022.[5] Employers ponied up cash bonuses and other inducements to recruits along with making efforts to offer elder and child caregiving help as part of their benefits packages. They are acknowledging that caregiving for aging parents, spouses, partners, and close relatives is a front and center concern for their workers. Based on my conversations with employers, workers, and benefits professionals, the issue is starting to garner attention.

Wellthy.com, for instance, a digital care concierge platform that helps employers assist staffers who have caregiving needs, is seeing growing interest for its services from US businesses. The company hires social workers as care coordinators and provides a technology platform to project-manage care, ranging from scheduling medical appointments to finding the right specialists to managing a move to a long-term care facility.

"I think it's a sea change," Lindsay Jurist-Rosner, Wellthy CEO and founder, told me when I interviewed her. Her firm's benefits are now offered by more than 600 businesses, and 700,000+ people have access to its services. "I think care considerations are going to become as common as 401(k) plans and healthcare coverage," Jurist-Rosner said. "If employers don't address [caregiving], then their employees are going to struggle to stay in their jobs or they're going to move to companies where they feel more supported."

Eldercare and other benefits have emerged as part of the new social contract prompted by the trends of longevity and population aging, according to a new Global Coalition on Aging report, "Employers' Role in the COVID-19 Environment: Winning in the Vastly Changed World of Work."[6]

"In a COVID-19 work environment, employers will need to increase focus on solutions for caregiving and financial wellness, which will take on heightened importance," the researchers found. "As employee needs have evolved, elder caregiving has joined childcare as a top benefit demand," Michael Hodin, CEO of the Global Coalition Aging, told me. "We see some changes in terms of offering employees benefits for elder caregiving." But, he added, "not as much as I think we will see over the next year or two."

But uncertainty has persisted. Even after vaccinations became widely available, the risk of Covid variants and outbreaks continued to loom, predominantly in areas with low vaccination rates. While some activities returned to normal, government officials and employers couldn't predict the future course of the pandemic; as a result, employers found it necessary to be flexible on policies for their workers.

OLDER WORKERS HANDLED
THE PANDEMIC BETTER

But here's the thing, and it's a biggie. Older workers were *not* as disturbed by the stress of the pandemic as their younger colleagues. "Our study found that older age groups were less worried about their mental health at work compared to their younger counterparts," Dan Schawbel, managing partner of Workplace Intelligence, told me. Eight in 10 Generation Z employees (age 22–25) in the workforce and 73 percent of millennials (age 26–37) said they've had more stress and anxiety at work than any year before, compared to 59 percent of baby boomers (age 55–74).

Well, of course, I thought when Schawbel shared those findings with me. Older workers have the benefit of experience in navigating sudden life shifts, including job losses, health scares, untimely deaths of loved ones, battering recessions, the shock of 9/11, and more. Life has equipped us with the resilience and understanding that comes with traversing those jolts.

Workers over 50 like you and me adapted. We learned to work from home offices like pros. And, believe it or not, some of us even thrived.

Many innovative small businesses and nonprofits run by senior entrepreneurs souped up their websites and pivoted to offering online sales and services to stay afloat.

Carol Nash is founder of Bernadette's House, a Maryland-based small nonprofit for girls age 8 to 17, which provides early intervention and prevention services through an after-school mentoring program. She reviewed the programs they were offering and took what they could online—from arts and crafts to Bible study.

Nash and her team crafted a streaming talk show, "House Talk for Teens," to examine important topics such as preparation for life after high school and the upside of having a mentor as you advance through your education. Meantime, a team of volunteers opened pathways for girls to be a part of Bernadette's House on such social media sites as Facebook, Instagram, Twitter, and YouTube.

"The way we do our business has changed. Even with the physical house open again, we intend to keep offering online programming," Nash explained to me when I reached out to her for a Next Avenue column on the ups and downs of entrepreneurs during the pandemic. Her facility has a capacity for only 20 girls, so the addition of the virtual platform ultimately reaches more girls with mentoring and homework help. Put that in the win column.

THE BIG QUIT

As a result of issues associated with the pandemic, droves of people departed their jobs voluntarily. They examined their priorities and happily took a chance on reimagining what they do for work. In fact, it's been dubbed the "Great Resignation" or the "Big Quit." They aren't looking back.

A Microsoft survey released in June 2021 revealed that 41 percent of the global workforce was planning on saying "see ya later" to their employers that year.[7] Many of these people were over 50 years old. Some were leaving for new beginnings with another employer; others wanted to pursue a dream endeavor; others stepped into retirement.

Of course, many workers over 50 who lost jobs during the pandemic didn't have that luxury of being financially secure enough to retire or to start over in a new career or business and are still on the sidelines. They are faced with the stark reality that the longer you're out of work, the tougher it is to land a new job.

AGEISM: A UNIVERSAL PROBLEM

While older employees showed their mettle in the pandemic, they came face-to-face with an age-old (forgive the pun) problem: ageism—discrimination against workers solely because of their age.

Hiring managers globally worry about the capabilities of people 45 and older to absorb new technologies and skills and to work with other age cohorts, even though research says the opposite. Eighty-seven percent of older employees perform as well, or better, than coworkers a decade junior.

These facts come from a research report, "Meeting the World's Midcareer Moment," published by Generation, a global employment nonprofit. In its 2021 report, Generation surveyed 3,800 employed and unemployed people as well as 1,404 hiring managers to uncover global employment trends in seven countries—Brazil, India, Italy, Singapore, Spain, the United Kingdom, and the United States.[8]

Generation's founder and CEO Mona Mourshed told me the research clearly showed that ageism is universal from culture to culture. Employers view just 18 percent of age 45+ job seekers as having the right experience for their entry and intermediate level roles. And only 15 percent are viewed as being a good "cultural fit" with their team.

One startling statistic: Of those surveyed who were unemployed, 63 percent of 45+ job seekers had been out of work for more than a year versus only 36 percent of job seekers 18–34.

Mourshed—who formerly led consultant McKinsey & Co.'s global education practice—said the report's findings show that hiring managers basically believe that workers over 45 have no strengths relative to the 18–34 and 35–44 age brackets.

Hiring managers are more apt to report that those age 35–44 have the best experience in terms of relevant education, relevant prior work, and the right technical skills for the job. But when you ask, "Well, what's the actual performance on the job of those who are midcareer and whom you've employed?," they respond that 87 percent are performing as well, if not better, than their younger peers and 90 percent are perceived as having stronger, or the same, retention potential as their younger peers.

One underlying reason for this disconnect: the majority of hiring managers participating in the survey were under age 45. Thirty-nine percent were 35–44, while 33 percent were 18–34, and only 28 percent were over 45. Quite likely, the younger hiring managers were prone to regard peers their age in general as more suitable and competent colleagues.

The researchers surveyed large, small, emerging markets, and culturally diverse countries—and the findings were 100 percent shared across the board, from industrial to service professions, from skilled trades to tech jobs.

The greatest amount of bias was found in tech professions. No doubt the widespread cultural belief that young people learn and adapt better to technology than older people was shared by the hiring managers in the survey.

In contrast, healthcare professions tend to be more accessible to older workers. One reason may be that when someone is involved in patient care and direct patient interaction, qualities like maturity and empathy are highly valued. And there is a bias that those who are midcareer are more likely to have those characteristics than those who are younger.

Ageism is entrenched in work culture. To change that ethos for older workers moving forward, age must be considered part of employer diversity, equity, and inclusion (DEI) missions and workforce mandates. An AARP 2020 survey found that more than half of the global organizations didn't include age as part of their definition of DEI.[9]

Statistics from AARP show that 78 percent of older workers say they have seen or experienced age discrimination in the workplace, the highest level since AARP began tracking this question in 2003.[10]

At an Indeed Interactive conference, a virtual event, Heather Tinsley-Fix, a senior advisor with AARP, told attendees that many older workers continue to feel marginalized by recruiters. "There are some professions, like healthcare, that do value experience, but overall, it's not great, and something we need to pay attention to."

Despite pervasive ageism, I'm optimistic about the big trends emerging postpandemic for older workers—more remote job opportunities, a rise in entrepreneurship or self-employment, a surge in career pivots, and a shift to more contract jobs that offer flexibility and work-life balance. Plus, a new emphasis on adult education and skill-building at older ages.

FIVE ENDURING WORKPLACE CHANGES

My far-reaching research **shows five noteworthy shifts** in the new workplace, as already mentioned. These will plainly impact the way you work, where you work, and what kinds of work you do at this stage of your life.

Working from Home Is No Longer a Perk

The great news is that employers discovered their remote workers performed well, and output and efficiency were on target with expectations. No beats were missed. Plus, working remotely cut operating costs for many of them.

The portion of job postings that make some reference to remote work on the job board Indeed.com has more than doubled since before the pandemic.[11]

Ladders, Inc., which analyzes data from 50,000 employers weekly, reported that in North America there were more than 80,000 remote jobs paying at least $100,000 in July 2021 as compared to 7,000 remote jobs available in March 2020. I expect that number to remain high in the years ahead.[12]

I'm a staunch proponent of working from a home office. I've done it for years. The increase and acceptance of remote work offers several paybacks that you might not have considered. When you aren't front and center in the office setting or standing alongside a colleague who is decades younger, you're more likely to be judged not by your graying hair or sagging neck, but on your merit and the results of your work.

For workers with age-related mobility issues who may struggle with a commute, working from home is a godsend. It also makes it possible to pursue jobs that might not have been realistic if an in-person presence was a prerequisite.

While I envision remote work as mainstream, a more likely model for many employers once the pandemic is contained will be a hybrid, more flexible workplace, with face time strategically clocked both in the office and at home.

"I don't think remote work will completely replace work at the workplace, especially for older workers," Richard Johnson, economist at the Urban Institute in Washington, DC, told me. "One of the attractions of work, especially for older people, is the social networks and camaraderie that it provides. Those are harder to maintain when most work is done remotely. But face-to-face interactions don't need to happen every day."

Contract Positions Are Swelling

The shift to contract or short-term projects can help you stay on the job or keep current work experience on your résumé while you hunt for a full-time position. It can also open the door at a potential employer that might lead to a full-time position. Employers are more apt to take a chance on an older worker in a contract position to avoid hiring a full-time employee with the full costs of benefits and what they might perceive as a high salary expectation.

Contract positions can also benefit someone who wants to keep earning a paycheck but doesn't necessarily want the "pedal to the metal" full-time commitment.

The downside, however, is if you depend on benefits that come from a full-time job, this trend can be disturbing. This is particularly an issue for workers in their 50s who rely greatly on an employer-provided retirement account and access to an employer-provided healthcare plan.

Midlife Entrepreneurship Is Increasingly Popular and Viable

Meet the new boss! It's you. In the new world of work, entrepreneurship will be a go-to solution for a growing number of adults over 50 who have either a burning desire to be their own boss or have grown disenchanted and discouraged by the job hunt and yearn to take control of their destiny.

The Kauffman Foundation, which studies entrepreneurship, saw a steep uptick in startup activity in 2020, with most of these new entrepreneurs 45 and older. Older entrepreneurs typically have more capital, knowledge, and experience than younger entrepreneurs and, as a result, a higher rate of success than their younger counterparts, according to a study by MIT researchers.[13]

Technology has made it possible to build a business without a bricks-and-mortar footprint and large startup costs. It also makes it seamless to hire a virtual helper on a contract or temporary basis rather than committing to the responsibility and ongoing overhead of full-time employees.

Dave Summers was one of those nouveau entrepreneurs in his early 60s. He was laid off as director of digital media productions at the American Management Association during the first rush of the pandemic in 2020. It was a shock, but he used it as an opportunity to start his own business as a digital media producer, coach, and animator creating podcasts, webcasts, and video blogs.

Summers and his wife also chose to relocate from Connecticut to Tennessee where the cost of living was lower. "My new work is all virtual, so I can live anywhere," he told me. "Not only is it a cheaper place to live, but we also love hiking and the outdoors, and our new town is in the foothills of the Great Smoky Mountains."

Older Workers Are Making Their Dream Career Changes

Career changes later in life used to make people gasp and question if you know what you're getting into, or if you have enough runway to really make a go of it in a new field. But the pandemic has infused people with a new desire, passion, and confidence. More and more, people are asking: If not now, when?

Hitting the Books Is a Smart Career Move

Lifelong learning is no longer just a great way to stave off boredom and pass the time or learn something you might have always wanted to study but didn't have time to. It's now an essential tool for staying up-to-date on your job or landing a new position when you are over 50. The good news is that the pandemic spurred an uptick in offerings of top-drawer and affordable adult education online.

Yes, there are risks and challenges to these broad trends for older workers, but I see the opportunities here, and I hope you will as well.

THE PACE OF CHANGE
HAS QUICKENED

All of these developments were occurring prior to the pandemic. I am not talking a revolution here. However, there's no question these changes have been fast-tracked as a result of Covid-19.

I don't believe everyone is going remote as the default position or all businesses will be remote, but when the pandemic is in our rear-view mirror there will be more remote and work-from-home openings than ever before.

There was already a movement to gig workers, consultants, short-term work, and contracts, and that's quickened.

People are living longer, healthier lives and working comfortably into their 70s and 80s, and that's the future reality. Hence, multigenerational workplaces will be the norm and employers will realize the upside of those kinds of synergies.

We have all learned new ways of doing our jobs. We've upped our tech savvy. We've paused and reflected on how we can bring meaning and purpose into our lives and how we might express those values in our work—starting *now*.

As Jeff Tidwell, CEO and cofounder of Next for Me (Nextforme .com), told me: "The pandemic has accelerated a movement to think of work and life in a more open-minded way. No matter the age, over the past year we rethought what work-life balance could be, including the time we spend with our families and communities, and even where we live."

The life is short phenomenon has taken flight. There has been psychological reset among almost everyone I know, especially the 50+ workers I've interviewed in recent months, about what makes a great job.

There are a myriad of reasons why our tolerance for working a job we don't enjoy has shifted. More than ever before, we realize the importance of how we spend our time. People dear to us died from a virus that terrified us. That shook us.

The pain was particularly sharp when we were unable to be alongside loved ones as they departed, look into their eyes, hug them, and say goodbye for a last time. I felt that sting when my friend since childhood, Janet, called to tell me her mom, Dr. Joanne Kuehner Robinson, had died of Covid-19 in an assisted care facility outside of Chicago. Janet hadn't been allowed to visit her mom for months due to the shutdown that banned visitors.

It broke my heart. In recent years, I was always working too hard to find the time to visit Joanne. I kept putting it on the back burner. And now she's gone.

Joanne was an important mentor to me as a young girl when there were few role models for women seeking careers. She was a working mom, medical doctor, and trailblazer in her field. When she graduated from the University of Pittsburgh School of Medicine in 1950, her class included seven women. She believed in me and motivated me to reach for the stars.

This unprecedented time has made us think hard about our priorities, particularly when there are more yesterdays than tomorrows ahead. We have been isolated, separated from friends and family for months on end. The experience has taught us lessons about what we value, what sustains us, and what it feels like to lose it.

In the context of our working lives and careers, all of this translates into understanding *why* working for a certain company, a nonprofit mission, or a boss should truly depend on being appreciated and respected for our effort and time. And we must return that feeling. It's nonnegotiable.

For some people this inner evaluation was unintentional, spurred by a job loss. For me, it was also the loss of a chunk of my income with the cancellation of in-person speaking engagements. I scrambled to fill that void with a plethora of writing assignments. While it was exhausting, I was grateful and felt fortunate to have the work. But I had to fine-tune my time management acumen and instill discipline and clearer communication with my editors more than ever before to keep things running smoothly.

We have been changed forever by the impact of the coronavirus on our lives, and so has our workplace.

HOW TO USE THIS BOOK

If you are a worker aged 50+, this is your handbook to take control of your professional life. I will share my expert advice as a career, personal finance, workplace futurist, and retirement strategist. That's my job, and this book is full of proactive things you can do.

My goals are to deliver action steps with hope and optimism. I come at this topic as someone who has been deeply immersed in the work and jobs field for decades—but also as one of you. I am in my sixth decade, self-employed as I write this chapter, and wrestling with the same challenges you are to stay relevant, add new clients, ride the current of the changes in my field, and so on. *I get it.*

I will discuss the key issues and questions facing older workers today and devote a chapter to each big shift in the new world of work:

- If you're unemployed, you'll learn ways to find a great new job.

- If you're currently employed, but uneasy about what is ahead, you'll learn how you can shift into a new and more satisfying role.

My aim is to keep it simple with proactive steps you can take away and make your own. There are plenty of good books on writing a riveting résumé, interviewing, and seeking out a successful second act. I have written a few myself.

In this book, you will discover the essence of succeeding in the new world of work, but I encourage you to seek additional resources for a deeper dive to learn more about these new and sometimes fast-changing trends. I will share some along the way.

Creating your best work life is a process. It requires commitment and patience. There's a wonderful Chinese saying, *mozhe shitou guo he*—"to cross a stream by feeling for the rocks with your feet." Take calm breaths and carefully proceed one rock at a time. You might feel a little wobbly or off-balance at times, but you'll get there with calm, cautiously placed, and steady footsteps forward to reach the other side.

Every so often, though, you will find yourself forced to make that leap to the next stony surface because it's your best—or perhaps your only—option. That's part of forging a stream and, metaphorically speaking, meeting all kinds of goals in life. Sometimes it does take a leap of faith. And you smile when you make it.

For me, the key to jumping with a horse, one of my passions, like crossing that stream, is that I must be fully committed. There's no room for hesitation. Yes, risk is involved, but I trust in my horse, my own capability, and my willingness to soar.

To find success in the new world of work, this is the attitude you must seek and then hold on to. Stay focused on your goal! Don't get sidetracked by allowing anxiety and the fear of rejection stop you from finding your dream job. You've got this.

It's showtime.

Why Older Workers Rock

Before I launch into the substance of your job search toolkit, I would be remiss not to review the biggest factor in getting a job these days for those of us over 50—*ageism*. Sadly, it is deeply embedded in our culture, and it's not going away. Myths endure about how older workers demand higher salaries than younger ones and cost organizations more in health insurance, or that they're not committed for the long haul and will retire as soon as they can start drawing Social Security or Medicare kicks in at 65.

Then there's the old chestnut about weak tech skills and reluctance to want to learn new ways of working, or not playing nicely with younger bosses or colleagues. These things generally aren't said aloud, but trust me, hiring managers I've talked to will admit it off the record. They don't want to take the risk.

While I see glimmers of employers coming to the realization that hiring someone who is older doesn't mean they are hiring someone with an expiration date, these bright spots are not the norm *yet*.

In the tight labor market that emerged in 2021, and challenged with an aging population, hiring managers began to shift their thinking.

They had to. The trend actually started prepandemic. While the massive impact of the shutdown economy in 2020 put a hard stop on that movement, it shifted back into gear with an improving economy.

As younger workers grab the remote working bar and merrily swing away from job to job chasing engagement, flexible hours, and higher pay, without a hint of remorse, employers are ever so gingerly acknowledging that older workers are, in fact, "qualified workers." The door is creaking opening for new hires over 50, and managers are discovering ways to retain experienced employees moving forward.

COLORADO SHOWS THE WAY

One of my favorite examples of a *with-it* state when it comes to embracing older workers is Colorado. The state has put in place a range of employment programs to connect employers with experienced workers over 50 and has trumpeted the business case for older workers. An increasing number of companies are participating.

Here's the business case:

- Experienced workers are not as likely to jump jobs than someone still gaining traction and climbing the workplace ladder.

- It costs more to hire than it does to develop current older employees. So, retaining experienced staff is vital to a company's bottom line.

- Older workers often want to be part of a team at this career stage, particularly those over 60. They are more than willing to say adios to the headache of being the boss or a manager. They're energized by working with a diverse crew of younger coworkers.

- Age diversity can make a big difference in an organization's performance. Studies have found that the productivity of both older and younger workers is higher in companies with mixed-age work teams. Each generation polishes the other. Everyone grows.[1]

You get the picture. Older workers *rock*. And Colorado knows that. The Rocky Mountain state now has the nation's second fastest growth rate of people 65+.

The Colorado initiative started prepandemic when employers in the state were having trouble hiring competent workers. So, Governor Jared Polis's office, helped by nonprofits in the state and private foundations, stepped in to convince employers to consider experienced workers as the solution. And it worked.

I was the keynote speaker for a webinar, *Age-Inclusive Management Strategies in Colorado.*[2] My topic, "Finding Work After 50 and Rethinking Retirement," was well-received, but for me, listening to the other speakers brought me hope about the improving prospects for older workers.

"There is much work to do to ensure that we don't waste talent and every Coloradan worker can reskill, upskill, and next skill to find a good career in our state as we recover from Covid-19 and prepare for the future work," Joe Barela, executive director of Colorado's Department of Labor and Employment, explained to the webinar audience.

"It's no longer appropriate, or acceptable, or even relevant, that we don't realize lifelong learning has to be something that both employers and government embrace," he said. "We need to make sure that our workforce has access to skills training that makes them relevant to the work of today and the future. We also know that as employers struggle to find talent that we need to look at different ways of how we prepare and recruit talent into the needed roles we have from hospitality to engineering, to construction to healthcare. The way that we do this is really focusing on skills-based hiring practices that will be a wave of the future."

Barela finished by saying that Colorado employers who don't actively recruit and retain older workers "will be put at a big disadvantage and lose out to competitors who have put thought and effort behind older worker recruitment and retention strategies. It's about more than recruiting and retaining older workers. It's about creating a better society, a society in which older people are not only seen, but fully appreciated for their talents and contributions."

Agreed.

Lee Wheeler-Berliner, managing director of Colorado Workforce Development Council, also chatted at the webinar about the push for job coaching for older workers, career navigation, and peer support groups that the state's workforce centers are offering.

I realize this is one state, one initiative. But I wanted to highlight it to spread the word of what I expect to see more of in the years ahead.

DON'T REJECT YOURSELF!

While we're making progress as a society in reversing the negative myths surrounding older workers and the ill-founded perceptions of many hiring managers, some older workers have internalized these myths and perceptions to their own detriment. Too many older workers believe they are less capable than younger people. At worst, some laid-off workers believe they're damaged goods.

If this describes your mindset, consider research conducted at Trinity College Dublin, which determined that older brains have key advantages:[3]

- Older adults find it easier to focus. When the research team asked subjects to complete a simple exercise that required sustained attention, they found the older set reported their minds wandering about 27 percent of the time. Younger people were daydreaming closer to half the time (47 percent).

- Older adults were less anxious. Young adults were constantly having to rein their attention back in, producing worry and stress. Older adults worked steadily and reported feeling much less anxiety.

- Older adults were in better control of their brains. "Our research suggests that older adults can be more focused, less impeded by anxiety, and less mentally restless than younger adults," commented Paul Dockree, lead researcher, in the report. The researchers suggest that as we age, our memory gets somewhat less reliable, so our brains compensate by learning to focus better on the task at hand.

No matter where you are in life, it's important to find ways to build your confidence—especially when you're confronting negative attitudes in other people. Pay attention and remember positive things about yourself and bright moments in your life. For me, it can be as simple as some positive feedback from an editor, or watching Elly, my dog, charge across an open field, which always makes me smile. And of course, never forget that healthy living and fitness imbue us with a can-do inner energy.

That translates into a *buoyant* self-awareness of who you are. Believing in yourself is the underpinning of confidence. And that, in turn, creates oomph to power your job search and muscle through the unavoidable unsettling emotions that can surface when you're met with rejections or dead-end pathways.

I was talking to my 91-year-old mom, Marguerite "Mugs" Hannon, before her death about this book and how I wanted to give people advice on landing a great job, and how hard it is for older workers to cope with the rejection that they often face. She quickly blurted out emphatically that her number one tip was: *"Don't reject yourself!"* And her number two tip was: *"Just try!"*

Mom's advice never gets old. She always did know best. And she's right, you've got to want to hire yourself. That's an opinion that you can absolutely control.

Lurking pessimism is that negative nelly in you that creeps out in those pesky mental conversations you have with yourself. We all stress about those myths about older workers that we've reviewed—and maybe even believe some of them. Stop the tape.

The remedy to cynical self-talk is to act. Do something. A tiny step or a weightier undertaking can make a difference. Send a résumé. Attend a webinar. Tweak your LinkedIn profile. Rehearse potential interview questions and your responses with someone. That's where the shift, the change, the forward motion begins.

Redirect your "it's hopeless" thoughts to a constructive catchphrase. Summon your inner moxie. You're the bee's knees. You're not too old for the job. Your experience makes you perfect for it. Tell yourself you *are* a rock star and believe it! Say it. Write it. Sing it.

Here's one of my favorite exercises to reframe your mindset for the job hunt at hand. This is for your eyes only, but utterly commit yourself to the process. Write your professional story and don't pull any punches.

Does that story dwell on the adverse things like losing out on a promotion or being fired or laid off? Let's change that language to focus on your wins, your successes. Keep your victory story in a place where you can read it regularly. You might include some of the feedback from your colleagues and past performance reviews as well. Pull

MY MANTRA

I have an "up" personal mantra I say aloud when I'm nervous about a work challenge, or as I walk to the dais before a speech, or before I turn the video camera on for a virtual presentation. I silently instruct myself, "Do the best that I can do right now." That's all we can do . . . our best right now.

out short snatches of those affirmations and print them out or handwrite and tape them where you will see them every day.

The words we tell ourselves become our reality, our experience, our future.

Stay present. When you are moving to a potential position and job, remember it's *today* and *tomorrow*, so you need to leave yesterday where it belongs. This is harder than you think it is. It's instinctual to answer questions with "back in the day" kind of responses from decades ago and not what you've done recently.

I have found myself doing this. Honestly, it does seem like *just* yesterday sometimes even though it was decades back. Ahh . . . "the collapse of time," as my dad always referred to the time warp of aging.

CONSIDER A COACH

To bolster your confidence and develop job-hunting strategies, you may want to hire a pro to guide you. Working with a career coach can be exceptionally helpful. An increasing number of employers are offering this help as part of their voluntary early retirement and severance packages. You might also attend a virtual workshop taught by a coach, or even take a class from one at a community college or connect with one through the career center at your alma mater.

So, how do you find a good career coach and the right one for you? One way is by asking friends and family. If your employer hasn't provided you with one, you also can do a Google or LinkedIn search for "career coach."

The International Coaching Federation (coachingfederation.org) provides a service to help you locate a coach with appropriate professional credentials. Other groups that provide access to coaches are the Life Planning Network (lifeplanningnetwork.org) and the Retirement Coaches Association (retirementcoachesassociation.org).

In today's world, there's no need to hire a coach in your backyard unless meeting in person is key to how you will get the most from it. Most coaches are accessible for online get-togethers or phone sessions. Hourly session fees can run anywhere from $85 to $300.

I advise interviewing three or four potential coaches before selecting one. He or she will be an integral part of your next step team, so it's well worth the time and effort to do your research. Most will provide one free session to get a feel for whether the two of you will be a good pairing.

To get the most from your sessions, consider in advance what services you're looking for. Do you need sensible advice about job searching, or nuts-and-bolts writing assistance with your résumé? Are you looking for someone to show you ways to squeeze your decades of work experience onto two pages, or to work alongside you to polish up your LinkedIn profile? Is it a coach who is skilled in the nuances of networking or a Sherpa to pull out for you what you really want in your next job by probing more personal and reflective subjects and giving you homework to complete these kinds of psychological exercises?

Coaches will undoubtedly ask if you have a financial plan and what your financial needs are in a new position. That's a key question, according to Dorian Mintzer, a retirement coach with Revolutionize Retirement. "I always say, no matter how much or how little money you have, it's important to figure out where does the financial piece fit in and how much money at this stage do you need to earn," Mintzer told me.

Finally, a career coach can be there to help sort through feelings of loss and grief that you may have from a job loss or decision to leave your longtime employer. "Even if it was you choosing to go, there's some grieving," she added.

More on all this in Chapter 5. But for now, and as you progress through the remainder of the book, I want you to remember the theme of this chapter—older workers "rock" and so do you!

3

Where the Jobs Are and Where They'll Be

I wish I could tell you definitively what jobs will be in hot demand for those of us over age 50 in the coming years, but I'm not a fortune teller. During the pandemic some job fields grew appreciably, while others shrank, only to recover or slip away entirely. There are new jobs emerging that you never heard of a few years ago, and with each passing year, technology, world health events, and climate change issues are creating new ones at a rapid pace.

Life has a way of whipsawing around us in a heartbeat. But there are a few broad industries that have been on the rise and are likely to continue to grow in the next several years, generating many new jobs. This roundup below is meant to get you thinking about the fields where there are likely to be openings now and in the years ahead.

The big picture is that workforce shifts may be grander in scale than had been projected before the pandemic, according to "The Future of Work After COVID-19" report by the McKinsey Global Institute.[1] Depending on how deeply these developments stick, the firm's researchers indicate that more than 100 million workers may find themselves changing occupations by 2030, a 12 percent increase worldwide from prepandemic levels. In more advanced economics, it may be as much as a 25 percent rise.

Noteworthy was the prediction that employers will make significant modifications in the way they look for new employees—focusing more on skills rather than academic degrees. If so, this could open a wider swath of jobs for those over 50. Google, Hilton Hotels, Ernst & Young, and IBM are among a bourgeoning number of employers that have already begun the process. Workers, however, will need to learn more technological skills to move into higher paying occupations, according to the research.

I would be remiss not to note that employers seek workers who fit their "preferred profiles" and gravitate to "workers currently in the role or in one related to it," according to "Hidden Workers: Untapped Talent," written by Joseph Fuller and Manjari Raman, from Harvard Business School, and Eva Sage-Gavin and Kristen Hines, from Accenture.[2]

Those workers are "more likely to have exposure to state-of-the-art technology and to have enjoyed employer-provided, vendor-supported training to build their skills," they wrote. "Employed workers thus gain an additional and increasingly large edge over those not employed. The latter struggle to know what skills to acquire, how and where to acquire them, and how to overcome their lack of financial resources and time to do so."

Bingo. This is a huge issue for older workers seeking new jobs. Spending to ramp up skills with no employer set to hire you or at least in your sights can be daunting and risky. And knowing what learning platforms or courses to tap to provide that education is another stumbling block, which can stop us from pressing on. (It's smart, if possible, to talk to graduates of certification programs or other skill-building courses to find out where they landed. Also, see if a program has employers who regularly seek to hire its graduates before you enroll.)

The Harvard Business School report explores the divide between companies allegedly incapable of finding qualified workers and "hidden workers" who don't get considered for open jobs. "Hidden" in this milieu means those working less than full-time who want to work full-time, those who have been unemployed for a long time, and those not working or currently seeking jobs but who could be drawn back into the labor pool.

Additionally, the researchers reported that "demand for humans with the more sophisticated skills to program or maintain numerically controlled machines and robots has surged." That is likely to continue. Accenture research found that 63 percent of executives report the pace of digital transformation for their organization is accelerating—"and 80 percent believe it is taking place at an unprecedented speed and scale," according to the study. "In the wake of Covid-19, with concerns for safety, social distancing, and the higher cost of protecting workers, evidence is gathering that employers are all the more inclined to employ automation to reduce manpower intensity in the future."

Enough gloom, here's the bright side. Change is inevitable and the rapid speed at which technology is transforming the workplace from the ways hiring is conducted to the jobs themselves is a moving target. That said, there are resources that can serve as a guide or North Star.

For me, the best place to get a sense of what is percolating in the broad job market is the analysis produced by the economists and researchers at the U.S. Bureau of Labor Statistics (BLS). It's my go-to, and I've spent hours poring over its highly regarded "The Occupational Outlook Handbook" (BLS.gov/ooh/). I recommend you do as well. This treasure provides a deep dive into industries, jobs, educational requirements, and pay, predicting the overall growth potential over the next decade.

Another terrific source to get a sense of jobs and industries on the rise is the "Career Exploration Tools" developed by the Occupational Information Network (O*NET) under the sponsorship of the US Department of Labor's Employment and Training Administration. It includes career assessment tools to help you consider job options, complete job applications, create résumés, and prepare for interviews and to shift fields.

These online tools can help you pinpoint work-related interests and what's a priority for you on the job. Then they can link you to nearly 1,000 occupations described by the O*NET database, as well as to occupational information in the Department of Labor's CareerOneStop (careeronestop.org/) resource center. The information spans the entire US economy. And the good news is that it's free and frequently updated from contributions by a broad range of workers in each occupation. You can tap into it at onetcenter.org/tools.html.

RIDING THE AGE WAVE

Now to the nitty-gritty. Not surprisingly, as we navigate the tough realities of an unparalleled health crisis brought into sharp focus by the coronavirus pandemic, the healthcare and social assistance sector is projected to add the most jobs, according to the BLS.

But the jolt of the virus and realization of how vulnerable the healthcare system is to future pandemics isn't the only factor driving healthcare and social assistance jobs. Boomers and Gen Xers are living longer lives than previous generations. And that translates to a swell in demand for home health and personal care aides, technicians, senior massage therapists, and other wellness health professionals.

These jobs are often for those in their 50s and 60s to provide services to those in their 70s, 80s, and 90s. These are jobs that I say are "riding the age wave." Among the fastest-growing healthcare occupations are physician assistants, nurse practitioners, physical therapists, and occupational therapy assistants.[3]

The pandemic also ramped up the awareness of mental health as people of all ages struggled with the loss of family and friends to Covid-19, burnout, disruptions in work, loss of jobs, and fear about the future.[4] Employment of substance abuse, behavioral disorder, and mental health counselors is on the rise, and that momentum is likely to continue for years. Jobs like behavioral healthcare manager, risk reduction manager, social worker, and case manager fall under this category. Titles include therapist, psychologist, counselor, and mental health clinician.[5]

JUMPING ON THE TECHNOLOGY BOOM

The growth in technology innovation and its impact on all aspects of our lives is the second big wave of future jobs. The Labor Department forecasts a surge of demand for people with information technology (IT) and computer-related skills, especially in cybersecurity, in the next 10 years. It expects job increases in IT support and telehealth.

Employment in computer and information technology occupations is projected to grow 13 percent from 2020 to 2030, faster than the average for all occupations. These occupations are projected to add about 667,600 new jobs. Demand for these workers will stem from greater emphasis on cloud computing, the collection and storage of big data, and information security, according to the forecast.[6]

These swelling positions include:

- Computer programmers who write and test code that allows computer applications and software programs to perform precisely.

- Computer support specialists who supply much needed help and advice to computer users and organizations.

- Computer systems analysts who analyze an organization's existing computer systems and find a solution that is more effective.

- Database administrators and architects who craft or shape systems to store and secure data.

- Information security analysts who can plan and carry out security measures to guard and protect an organization's computer networks and systems from hackers. Cybersecurity, as you know, is all the buzz and for good reason, given the high-profile and widespread security breaches we've faced here in the United States and globally that have resulted in serious economic impacts including food and gasoline shortages.

- Network and computer systems administrators responsible for the day-to-day operation of computer networks, web developers, and digital designers.

- Software developers who design computer applications or programs as well as software quality assurance analysts and testers who identify problems with applications or programs and report defects.

FASTEST-GROWING JOBS

While there is a range of occupations to keep an eye on for opportunities between now and 2030, the following are among the fastest-growing ones, according to the BLS:

- Wind turbine service technicians: 68 percent growth rate

- Solar photovoltaic installers: 52 percent growth rate

- Cooks and restaurant workers: 49 percent growth rate

- Agents and business managers of artists, performers, and athletes: 46 percent growth rate

- Exercise trainers and group fitness instructors: 39 percent growth rate

- Makeup artists, theatrical and performers: 37 percent growth rate

- Statisticians: 35 percent growth rate

- Animal caretakers: 34 percent growth rate

- Information security analysts: 33 percent growth rate

- Film and video editors: 33 percent growth rate

OTHER RAPIDLY GROWING JOBS

Pockets of the manufacturing industry are geared to bump up. Employment in the pharmaceutical and medicine manufacturing industries, for instance, is anticipated to grow by about 19 percent in the next decade. And the upswing in remote work will lead to an increase in computer and peripheral equipment manufacturing jobs over the coming decade, according to the BLS.[7]

Another field with strong jobs growth is scientific and medical research. An increasing number of jobs linked to future pandemic preparedness will emerge. The Labor Department foresees sharp demand for biological technicians, medical scientists, biochemists, biophysicists, and epidemiologists.

Employment in media and communication occupations is projected to grow 14 percent from 2020 to 2030, faster than the average for all occupations, resulting in about 151,500 jobs. This is good news to my ears. Jobs include broadcast, sound, and video technicians who set up, operate, and maintain the electrical equipment for media programs as well as editors who strategize, critique, and modify content for publication. In addition, interpreters and translators will find a growing number of openings, as will public relations specialists. Also in demand: technical writers who produce instruction manuals, how-to guides, journal articles, and other supporting documents to explain complicated and technical information more simply.

Occupations in business and financial operations are estimated to grow 8 percent from 2020 to 2030, adding about 750,800 jobs. Globalization, a budding economy, and a convoluted tax and regulatory environment will lead to strong demand for accountants and auditors. In addition, increasing usage of data and market research to understand customers and product demand, and to evaluate marketing tactics, will result in a growth for market research analysts.

Meantime, work in education, training, and library occupations is projected to grow 10 percent from 2020 to 2030, adding approximately 920,500 jobs. Student enrollment is forecast to surge; consequently, postsecondary teachers and preschool, elementary school, and secondary school teachers will be necessary to meet the demand. One caveat: education, training, and library occupations are determined by state and local budgets, and budgetary limits may check job growth.

Employment in food preparation and serving-related occupations is projected to grow 20 percent from 2020 to 2030, much quicker than the average for all occupations, generating about 2.3 million jobs. The impetus: population and income growth will result in bigger consumer demand for food at a range of dining establishments and grocery stores.

There's your smorgasbord of possibilities to consider, and certainly there are hot spots in many industries not mentioned here. Consider this wide-ranging perspective a teaser and a general overview to stimulate your ideas about what interests you, what your current skill set might suit, and where you'd like to explore as you formulate a way forward to succeed in the new world of work. It's a launching pad. Let's now move on to put the rest of the pieces in place for piloting your path to work that you love and that pays the bills.

Taking Control of Your Future

Now that you know the general landscape of the new world of work for those of us over 50, it's time to take stock of what's important to you, consider the options, and make a plan, so you can take control of your future.

This is the fun part, in my opinion. You begin with journaling and self-exploration exercises. If you don't like the idea of scribbling in a notebook or typing on a computer, I suggest calling out the artist in you and making a drawing or map of your answers with a marker and poster board. You can even pick different color markers for each topic. Each question can have its own branch on a tree. Some may intertwine. Call it your Job Map or your Life-Planning Map. It might not be tidy. But the process will open doors for you.

Dream a little. Give yourself permission to brag (at least to yourself) about what you're *really* good at, and to be creative.

It's liberating.

This personal examination is super helpful when it comes to finding a job that is a fit for you and you for it. This is your individual road map.

No two paths to finding a great job are the same. So, while I can give you the lay of the land, it's up to you to identify what makes your experience and talent stand out and select the type of work that will allow you to be happy and to prosper.

There is no magic elixir, yet the very action of sleuthing and making yourself truly think about what you want and what you have to offer, no matter how small, is what allows the shift to something new to begin.

Of course, such simple heuristics are not without their risks. You may start down some lanes of exploration that aren't going to work for you. But it's that trial-and-error approach that can yield some surprising results.

When you sit back fearful of rocking the boat or drawing attention at your present job even though you feel stuck and overlooked, or passively wait for a response to a virtual job application, or expect a new direction to suddenly present itself, you set yourself up for frustration and disappointment.

Take back the power. It will, however, take a genuine willingness to be honest with yourself and a little time and effort. You're worth it.

WHERE ARE YOU NOW?

The first step is the simplest. What phase of your career path are you on today? If you're 51, chances are what you're looking for is quite different than someone who is 67.

Are you nearing retirement? Retired and looking for a retirement job? Hunting for a remote position? Seeking ways to stay relevant in your current role, or want to keep climbing to higher-paying positions and responsibilities? Considering a career transition? Dreaming about being your own boss? Interested in shifting to nonprofit work to segue your corporate expertise to bolster a cause you believe in?

These are big picture questions, so take some time to really sit and consider them.

Then dig a little deeper. What's your *purpose*? I know you hear that buzzword all the time, but the truth is, it gets to the core of what you're looking for in the workplace. Feeling joy in the work we do is important to our sense of worth and identity. I believe it's the biggest contributor to our success on every level.

It's more important than the money you make.

If you don't know why you want a certain job or why you want to start your own business, you won't do the work necessary to get hired or to build a profitable business. Your business will likely fail, or if you go the employment route, you'll likely wind up in a position you resent, working for an employer that you don't appreciate and who doesn't value you.

What is your "why you *do* what you *do*"? This goes deeper and is more profound in some ways than your overall purpose because it's not so dreamy. It's stark and practical. Before you launch a serious job search, articulate a clear vision and understanding of what it is that inspires you, gets your eyes twinkling, and your energy pumped— your *mission*.

People have mission statements. These are not just for businesses and nonprofit organizations. Mine is taped to the shade of the lamp that sits on my office desk. It reminds me why I love my job and when to say no to certain assignments or pass on a potential client. My mission statement makes me feel in control. And so will yours.

Why do *I* do this? Why do I do the writing I do and the speaking? It's because I want to touch people's lives with hope and contribute to their success and well-being. So, for me, my *why* is to *make a positive difference in someone's life*. I want to give people the tools to feel confident about their personal finances or show them how they can fall in love with their job again, or offer them a kit of advice they can use to land a great job—that's my mission.

Start a Journal

Journaling about my mission and ambitions helps me feel self-confident and view myself as a successful expert. It will provide that same ballast to you as well.

Tease out as many specifics as you can about your career goals and why realizing those goals would be good for *you*, and even better, good for the world around you.

You're one decision away from changing your life, so be clear about what you want. Write down a list of the reasons why you're looking for a job. Then drill down through the ins and outs of it in your *ideal* world—from the hours you'll work, to the tasks you'll do, to the type of workplace you'll enjoy.

Give yourself a deadline. Maybe it's the journalist in me, but I find a deadline, even one that is self-imposed, pushes you to get going. It imposes discipline. And it can kick up the adrenaline that can bring out the best in you.

Nancy Collamer, retirement coach, founder of mylifestylecareer .com, and expert on second-act career trends, encourages her clients to ask these primary questions: Who or what energizes you? And who or what drains you?

I like that approach. Your answers will fire up your job search. I also suggest asking: What is it you've loved about past jobs, even the one you might have right now? And what has made you miserable?

Some more questions for you to explore in your journaling: What makes you cry for joy? What brings tears of sorrow? These causes or events tell you a lot about what moves you emotionally and will help you get to the root of your *why*.

If you're looking to switch careers, why do you do what you do now? And why do you want to move in another direction?

What kind of hours do you want to devote to your new job: full-time, part-time, contract, seasonal, or flexible?

Who would be your dream employers? Create a list of companies or nonprofits that you admire for their mission or their products or services. I recommend keeping it to your top 10 choices.

If you get through to an interview, a hiring manager will sense your passion for the company—if it's genuine—and want you on the team. It's also flattering in a subliminal way. It makes hiring managers feel good about their own decision to work there. That's a hidden check in the pro column for you. Human nature.

Take no more than five minutes and jot down jobs you would truly enjoy doing and could realistically qualify for or could ramp up the prerequisite skills for without too much cost or hassle. By doing this quickly, you don't get too deep into the weeds. The ones that jump into your head are your go-tos, at least initially. This will narrow your job search and give you a running start to land a job where you will be engaged and happy.

What Are Your Strengths?

Examine your existing skill set and work experience, looking for patterns about the kind of work you value and that enriches you. This can be from jobs you had years ago, so don't get stuck on the most recent ones. You might even ask people in your inner circle to send you an email with some attributes they recognize in you that you may take for granted. These are all clues to the kind of work you might investigate.

Explore the softer, or what I like to call human, skills in your wheelhouse. Do you see yourself as curious, resilient, willing to try new things, a leader, a great communicator? Be truthful. You might prefer to stick to the road more traveled where you don't need to be a beginner again. Own that. Not everyone wants a bold new challenge and that's OK.

If you need help categorizing your strengths, one useful resource is the CliftonStrengths assessment. I also recommend taking the official Myers-Briggs test (mbtionline.com) or a comparable free questionnaire suggested by psychologists at 16personalities.com. These kinds of tests can help you put into words what your best qualities are, such as practical, imaginative, enterprising, innovative, pragmatic, or problem-solver.

What Do You Enjoy?

Consider what you like to do for fun, hobbies, or sports. These activities reveal things about the kind of activities that turn you on and that you excel at in some fashion. In turn, they also expose a skill set that translates to the work you do. I have found that what it takes to perform a hobby or a sport successfully is usually in line with the challenges you face on the job in some respect.

For me, showing in a top-ranked equestrian competition in a large arena over a course of eight jumps when it's just me and my horse, Caparino Z, in front of an audience-filled grandstand is pretty much like giving a keynote speech. It demands focus, memorization, rhythm, relaxation, grace under pressure, and expertise. (I do think it's harder.) And it's a little like writing for me, too. Smoothly putting the pieces of a course together one jump at a time is like organizing an article, or a book, one paragraph or one chapter at a time.

When I'm in the ring, I feel like I have control because I'm doing it on my own. That's why taking the time to work through some of these backstage exercises makes a difference as you chart your next step. They put you in control of your job search and ultimate work satisfaction.

Now it's your turn. What does your passion for chess or gardening or sailing tell you about yourself? Or playing the piano or tennis? You see where I'm going here.

Try it. It's pretty simple to find those clues. They're what turns you on, what energizes you, and what you're good at. It's something that you would do even without earning a paycheck from it.

Say sailing is your passion. Sailing involves constant decision-making and problem-solving, an ability to make last-minute moves under pressure if the weather shifts. That's a hint to what excites you. These signs will evolve into career ideas. You'll see the connections to what you may want to look for in your next position.

When Keith Cooper, who had a background in tech sales, began looking for a new sales position in his 50s, he found the market wanted people in that role who were much younger than he was. Much to his delight and surprise, when he landed a new job as a project manager for a midsized logistic company, it was his sailing acumen honed for decades that sealed the deal.

"Being a project manager is like moving something from point A to point B," he told me. "I do that with a sailboat on journeys. I told my boss, who I met while sailing together and heard about the job opening, 'I'm not a project management professional. I don't have the training.' And he said, 'Well, I'm not really concerned about certification or training. I need somebody that can get things done.' I said, 'Well, you know from sailing together I definitely can get things done.'"

YOU BET YOUR LIFE

Steve Dalton, who gives job-hunting advice to students as program director for daytime career services at Duke University's Fuqua School of Business, has an exercise that will help you cut to the chase. He calls it the "You Bet Your Life" exercise (it takes one minute). Select one professional skill you're confident you're in the top 1 percent of the world. Have some swagger here. At the very least, you should seek out a job that will let you use it! By swiftly identifying your top skill, it "just clarifies everything," Dalton told me.

What's Your Vision?

Create a vision board. This can be physical on a poster board or virtual on your computer with an app like The Landing (thelanding .app). It will contain images that symbolize what your goals are, what success means to you, and what motivates you.

Add catchphrases that resonate with you, or pictures of what's possible in your life right now because you're working and earning money. These can be corny, but who cares? You're the only one looking at it.

Some of mine are:

- People Pay to See People Who Believe in Themselves
- Do It with Passion or Not at All
- These Are Great Days
- Those Who Don't Believe in Magic Will Never Find It
- Life Isn't About Finding Yourself, It's About Creating Yourself

Place your vision board where you bump into it regularly. It can be your screen saver or taped to your closet door or refrigerator. It's a cue that will help you stay the course. But don't let it go stale; it's always a work in progress. Play with it and make changes as you get more clear-eyed about where you're headed. Add images, move them around, or jettison them completely. Have some fun with it!

Let it rip. No one is going to judge you.

THE REWARDS OF STAYING IN THE WORKFORCE

Did you accept an early retirement package in recent years? Many of you might have as employers spooked by the pandemic sought to lighten payrolls and the 50+ set had a target on its back.

Were you laid off and decided, enough, let's call me *retired*? You simply didn't have the energy or the heart to get back on the job hunt trail at this stage and face the ghosting and rejection that inevitably are part of the scene these days for older workers.

Were you a member of the Great Resignation nation, or what I like to call the Great *Reimagination*? You had plenty of time to figure out that, "Hey, I really hate my job and I have no interest in going back to the office. I'm out of here to find something different."

Well, if you're reading this book, I suspect you're having a change of heart or you need to continue working in some fashion. That's a good thing, a really good thing. Here's why. We're living longer, healthier lives and that means we have more years of living to finance.

The financial safety net from paid work is a huge factor to healthy aging. The more years you fund your retirement plans, the stronger your future financial security and the less stress and anxiety you have over money issues.

Second, when you're earning income, you may not need your Social Security benefit, so you have the ability to delay taking it, boosting your eventual payout. Start collecting Social Security at age 70, and your monthly check will be more than 30 percent higher than if you begin benefits at 66—and 76 percent more than if you start taking benefits at 62 (when most people do).

Third, earning a paycheck can help you keep your hands off your existing retirement accounts such as a 401(k) or an IRA, allowing the funds to keep growing tax-deferred until, by law, you need to begin to take distributions. You generally are required to start taking withdrawals from your IRA, SEP IRA, SIMPLE IRA, or retirement plan account when you reach age 72. Roth IRAs do not need withdrawals until after your death. You might even be able to keep socking more funds away in these accounts.

The fourth financial motive to stay on the job is that it provides income to help pay for health insurance until you're eligible for Medicare at 65. In 2021, as someone who is self-employed, I paid more than $800 a month for coverage in Washington, DC. Enough said.

The number of employers offering their retired workers medical benefits is dwindling, and those who do are increasing the amount retirees must contribute to the cost of coverage—another reason to stay employed or to find a job that offers you access to a health plan.

For women, working beyond the customary retirement age can deliver financial security from the very real threat of poverty in their 80s.

"Financial problems in retirement and senior debt arise with insufficient income as a result of lower lifetime earnings and less in savings, costs of family caregiving, and divorce," Cindy Hounsell, the founder and president of the Women's Institute for a Secure Retirement (Wiser.org), told me. Wiser is a nonprofit organization dedicated to women's financial education and advocacy.

Money aside, you may want to stay on the job because it's good for your mental health. Work provides purpose and human connection. That's a psychological and emotional win that's hard to put a number on.

Work also has the power to keep you mentally sharp. Research studies have shown that cognitive performance levels drop quicker in countries that have younger retirement ages. "Use it or lose it" and staying engaged in the workplace can stave off some forms of dementia, researchers have found.[1]

In the following chapters we'll explore the various options for older workers from staying at the same job to looking for a new job in the same line of work, contract/gig work, transitioning to a different career, and entrepreneurship.

Regardless of how you move forward, though, if you want to take control of your future work life, it's important to build a foundation of fitness. Now that we've run your inner MRI as I like to call it, and I've made my case for the incentives of staying in the workplace, here are some action steps that are totally under your control.

KERRY'S FITNESS PLAN

This fitness regimen is truly at the spine of my career strategy program for workers over 50, but let's face it, it's good for practically anything you want to do in life.

Here are the three elements:

- Financial fitness

- Physical fitness

- Spiritual fitness

Keys to Financial Fitness

When you're financially strong, you have choices about the life you live and the work you do—whether it's for compensation or pro bono, full-time or part-time. You're nimble. Financial fitness gives you the independence to pursue the kind of work you may have put aside earlier in your life because it didn't offer the income and advancement you needed at that time.

It opens possibilities. You may be able to accept a job you truly love even if it pays a fraction of what you once earned. That's because you aren't locked into earning a certain salary in order to pay the monthly bills.

This financial freedom allows you to experiment, try some different things, start over in a second act, start a business, say yes to a contract gig, and on down the line.

This is a progression and takes time, so be patient with yourself. The best way to begin is to craft your budget. This gives you a snapshot of how you spend your money and even your time. Begin by writing down your recurring fixed expenses, such as your mortgage or rent payment, health insurance premiums, utilities, and so forth.

Last year's outlays can provide a guide. Pull out your most recent tax return for some guidance. Where can you trim? Are there some expenses from the past year that you can cut back?

Jot down optional expenses even if you don't know exact amounts, such as groceries, restaurants, and entertainment. Of course, there will be inevitable costs, such as unanticipated medical bills, veterinary charges for a family pet, or auto or home repairs.

Be diligent about saving. I recommend a cushion of six months or more of living expenses in cash or cash equivalent funds set aside for sudden emergencies, especially if you're preparing to make a career transition, whether to a new field of work or to follow a dream.

Do a review of your credit report. The three big credit bureaus—Experian, TransUnion, and Equifax—provide everyone with one free credit report annually. Request one at AnnualCreditReport.com. When you get it, look for mistakes. Even something as simple as a misspelled name on an entry or confusion with someone who has a similar name can dip your credit score.

Your credit score is determined in part by your credit report. Don't ignore it. It impacts your total financial and, in turn, work life. Here's why: If you need to borrow funds to start your own business, lenders use it to decide whether they should loan you money and what your interest rate will be. Landlords may use it when deciding whether to rent to you. And if you're switching to a new firm, many employers evaluate it when determining whether to hire you.

The most obvious way to keep your score in shape is to correct mistakes on your credit report and pay your bills on time. Neglect a pay date, and your score drops big-time. All it takes is one late payment to squash your score.

If you find a mistake, contact the credit bureau or bureaus where you noticed the error and explain the inaccuracy in writing. Next, write the company that provided the information to the credit bureau. A credit bureau typically has 30 days after getting a dispute to examine and verify information with the company that furnished it. Then it must report back to you within five days of concluding the inquiry.

Pay off any high-interest credit card debts, college loans, and auto loans. This doesn't happen in a snap of the fingers, but if you're disciplined you can tackle this one and take a good thwack at bringing them down. Debt is a dream killer. When I talk to people who want to change careers or start a new business, money is always the biggest stumbling block.

It may make sense to move to a smaller home, especially if your kids have launched, or even to relocate to a town with a lower cost of living. You might be able to use the proceeds from the sale of your bigger digs to pay cash for your new place and be mortgage-free. Of course, relocating is a little thornier if you have a family to consider. But in the new world of remote work, it can be a real cost-saver for you.

Moving is kind of radical, I know. If that's not in the cards for you, and you are still paying down a mortgage on your home, explore refinancing to a lower interest rate. Figure out how much you can save over time with an online refinancing calculator at sites like Bankrate.com and HSH.com.

Review your overall financial health including investments, assets, retirement plans, and debts. You might start by hiring a financial advisor if you don't already have one on your team. He or she can help answer your questions and lend a sharp eye to your total financial picture.

For unbiased guidance, look for a fee-only planner with the Certified Financial Planner designation. You can find one by visiting the websites of the National Association of Personal Financial Advisors (napfa.org), Financial Planning Association (onefpa.org), or Certified Financial Planner Board of Standards (CFP.net).

Keys to Physical Fitness

Step two of my fitness plan is physical fitness. I know it's hard to see why that matters when you are looking for how to succeed in the new world of work, but it is a big factor. Often, older job seekers ask me: Should I have Botox? Should I dye my hair? I say, not really. If it makes you feel better, go for it. But what you really need to do is get your body tuned up. It's totally your call about the other expensive procedures.

When you're physically fit, you have the energy, positivity, and can-do spirit that comes from fitness. You feel good, and it shows. It goes a long way to fighting back ageist stereotypes of not having the stamina or grit for the job.

Hiring managers, bosses, and colleagues can't identify what it is about you, but they want what you have. They want you on their team. That fitness translates to a vibe that is catching and empowering, and concerns about age slip away without them even realizing it.

I'm not talking about running speedy miles, mind you, but walking 20 minutes a few days a week, swimming, or doing some other fitness routine you like. I'm also speaking about eating with an eye to nutrition and health.

I walk my Labrador retriever several miles a day, but there are lots of things you can do. Build that into your schedule.

Keys to Spiritual Fitness

Spiritual fitness is the third leg of my fitness plan. I'm not referring to traditional religious practices, rather I'm suggesting finding an approach to center you and bring balance and confidence to your working world as well as your personal life and journey.

Specifically, consider activities such as mindful mediation, ikebana (the spiritual Japanese art of flower arrangement), tai chi, or Qigong (pronounced "chee-gong"), an ancient Chinese exercise and healing technique that involves meditation, controlled breathing, and movement exercises. These kinds of actions deliver a ballast, a source of strength to weather the stresses that can come with job hunting or starting and running your own business. It's a private inner space where you can go to quiet the noise, refresh, and give yourself the inner focus to keep moving forward as you pursue your next career goal.

The HOVER Method

To wrap up this chapter on exercises and habits that will help you feel in control of your working life, I want to share my HOVER method. I frequently share it with the audiences I speak to and regularly refer to it in my writing. Like Kerry's Fitness Plan, it will empower you in the weeks and months ahead.

HOVER stands for hope, optimism, value, enthusiasm, and resilience.

Hope is believing that you can grasp your goals, and you will find a way. *You are your own best hope.* Take some time and let this sink in. Remind yourself of this. Maybe add it to your vision board slogans. Only you can make a lasting impact, navigate a shift, and change how you experience your new path.

Optimism is the juice. This is a central feature in loving what you do every day, jumping over obstacles and naysayers, and navigating a job search. When you're optimistic, you have a feeling of enthusiasm that you can lean into, that pushes you to act and to see opportunities and solutions to difficulties. It keeps you picking up the phone asking for help and advice. It keeps you from shutting down when the job hunt is a struggle, or your current job feels like a dead end.

This can-do approach lets you bounce back quicker after rejection and not feel the urge to toss in the towel and back away from a challenge. It also unlocks your eyes to grasp how "you *can*" bring about change, and not focus on how "you *can't.*"

Optimism is about feeling good about what lies ahead. My husband teases me about being an upbeat kind of gal, but I'm not naïve. I take a glass-half-full attitude and tend to surround myself with those who do as well. I am, however, keenly aware of the other half of this illusory glass.

I'm this way because I have chosen to be. I choose to center my efforts and attention on the fullness of the glass. Some people discuss this as the silver lining in the cloud. You decide.

You control how you choose to frame your mindset. From my experience, those who succeed are the ones who recognize both sides exist but opt to draw energy from the half-full glass.

One way to develop optimism is to pay attention to what's going fine in your life and stop dwelling on what's going wrong—or potentially might. It can be as simple as writing down or conducting a mental recap in your head each night of three good things that went down that day. It might be as esoteric as seeing a rainbow or as ordinary as a meal shared with friends or positive feedback on a work project.

Optimism also comes from gratitude. Habitually taking stock of the concrete things you like the most about your job or life can build this muscle. Give yourself a moment or two to be grateful for whatever those things are daily.

Value means having the inner poise to know that if you make the effort, you'll get results or see growth. It means you personally value the significance of your own work, skills, and talents. It means you believe in yourself. Sorry. I know that's a cliché. But it is true.

When you have that inner direction and self-confidence that doesn't depend on what others say or think about you—that will guide your actions. It's subtle, but those around you will feel and react to it.

One way to shape your sense of value is to persistently learn and add to your wheelhouse. To deal effectually with change and to create transformation in your work life, keep evolving yourself.

The most creative and resourceful people I know are constantly taking classes or going to lectures or working on self-improvement. It's enjoyable, and when you're gaining knowledge, you observe the world around you in new ways. You see things. You listen more closely. Your mind opens to let fresh ideas in.

Enthusiasm is the indefinable spice that lifts your energy and helps you forge through changes, both internal and external. It is a contagious force, almost like a superpower, that is hard for those you work for and with to ignore. An eagerness to try new things, take a risk, and see the upside of a project can lead you to stimulating assignments and opportunities that will bring happiness to your work life.

Resilience, or a capability for bouncing back from a setback, a job loss, or rejection, is vital to achieving happiness in your work, staying in control, and succeeding in the new workplace. When you're resilient, you are hardwired to ride out workplace changes, pivot, and turn them into prospects.

Resilient people avoid the impulse to get stuck in the past. They're curious. They keep learning, asking questions, and pushing to stay current. Resilience is something you can acquire. One way is by constantly learning new things. When you learn new things, you are a beginner again. You might even fail at first, or not be a star student, but then you get it. It clicks, and you're off.

What I have discovered throughout my career is that when I learn something in one area it can help me in another. For instance, what I learn in riding lessons from my trainer translates to my work life even if I'm not consciously aware of it. The big ones that I constantly need to be reminded of are to be patient, don't rush, and always communicate with my horse.

In recent years, Gayle Williams-Byers, a South Euclid Municipal Court judge, has taken a range of classes and workshops from horseback riding lessons to online classes in American Sign Language offered by Gallaudet University in Washington. "I don't have a reason to use these things in my professional life, but learning helps me to focus better," she shared with me. "It's also something that I have some control over. I take classes in subjects I am just wildly interested in learning about it.

"When I expand my brain, my wingspan is greater. It lets you get a little higher, to get above the headwinds."

Job-Hunting Strategies

Want to know one of the biggest obstacles to landing a job? Automated-hiring technology rejects countless people from job consideration. While this software (known as an application tracking system) isn't new, its use has accelerated in recent years and has been fine-tuned to cull out the hundreds of applications and résumés employers often receive electronically for a single open position.

Workers of all ages who are unemployed, underemployed, or working part-time *want* to get hired for full-time jobs, but the hiring methods discard their applications because they don't fit the strict criteria in the job description, even though they could productively perform the job.

I hear this all the time when interviewing workers over 50, and I have experienced this myself.

Perpetual advancements in technology are acutely changing the nature of the job hunt in the new world of work, and will continue to do so. It has made it much easier to learn about job openings through online job boards, but the underbelly is that it's made it harder than ever to break through the clutter and competition to get noticed.

It's common for more than 300 résumés to be submitted for a job posting. When companies use software to screen résumés, up to 50 percent of those applications never get seen by a person, according to recruiters I interviewed.

These systems represent the foundation of the hiring process in a majority of organizations. In fact, more than 90 percent of employers in the Harvard Business School survey mentioned in Chapter 3 (comprising 8,000 hidden workers and more than 2,250 executives across the United States, the United Kingdom, and Germany) use automated screening to initially filter or rank potential middle-skills (94 percent) and high-skills (92 percent) candidates.

Employment gaps in your résumé, for instance, send you to the dismissed bin. And that has serious repercussions for caregivers and working mothers who had to step out of the workforce during the pandemic. This phenomenon has been building.

"Over the last few decades, the rising burden of care—both childcare and eldercare—has led people either to drop out of the workforce altogether or seek part-time work," according to the Harvard report.[1]

This is especially true for job seekers who are 50+ as well as ones who've taken time out of the workforce due to family caregiving responsibilities. Nearly 2 in 10 employed family caregivers have had to quit their jobs over the course of caring for a loved one, according to a Rosalynn Carter Institute for Caregivers national survey, "Working While Caring."[2]

Employers are aware of the consequences on both sides of the hiring process. Roughly 9 of 10 executives queried by the researchers said they are fully aware that the software they use to screen applicants stops them from seeing potentially great candidates. According to the study, the practice results in more than 10 million workers never even having a chance to interview for a job.

OVER-BLOATED JOB DESCRIPTIONS

What's the disconnect? Applicants are cast off for a variety of factors. It's not only time out of the workplace. Frequently, a résumé lacks the precise words to match the job qualifications and responsibilities listed in the job posting.

Moreover, these wish lists ask for everything under the sun and more. I personally get exhausted reading these swollen descriptions in the online postings from employers and wonder what super human can possibly juggle all these responsibilities and the myriad of qualifications required.

"It's all about what's a nice to have versus need to have," Harvard's lead researcher for the study Joseph Fuller told me. "They put lots of hurdles in there. And the system values those who have the credentials that are marketable now, and it discredits—or puts much lower emphasis on experience—miles on the tires, if you will."

There are also screening filters that skip over applicants without college degrees. "A degree is not the same thing as a skill," said Ramona Schindelheim, editor in chief of WorkingNation (workingnation .com), a nonprofit focused on helping Americans get jobs and stay employed.

"Your experience as a problem-solver or a leader isn't determined by a piece of paper," she told me. "These are qualities that you can only 'sell' in an in-person interview by sharing examples of how you fixed an issue, came up with a creative solution, or encouraged and mentored a team member to help her or him realize their potential. If you don't even bother to talk to someone who, say, hasn't worked in the past six months, you might be missing out on all they can bring to the table."

Applicant tracking systems and digital challenges can put you at a disadvantage in the future world of work. But there are ways you will learn to meet these. Some of those methods are shared below.

At a more granular level, though, the atmosphere is, for lack of a better word, murky in the new world of work, even if you do manage to squeak through the automated e-screeners. Some employers embrace experienced workers. Others not so much. I wish I could say hands down, read this book, especially this chapter, and you're golden. You'll master the black hole of the problems, jobs you are trained to do will suddenly appear, and all will be well.

There is some potential good news here. Some of the largest US companies are involved in an effort launched in 2021 to prevent artificial intelligence software from triggering discriminatory results.

The Data & Trust Alliance (dataandtrustalliance.org) developed "Algorithmic Bias Safeguards for Workforce" and has signed up employers across a range of industries, including American Express, CVS Health, Deloitte, General Motors, Humana, IBM, Mastercard, Meta (the parent company of Facebook), Pfizer, Nike, and Walmart to work together to weed out algorithmic bias and prevent artificial intelligence software from triggering discriminatory results.

I concede that there's not a cookie-cutter playbook that fits all ages and desires. I do, however, have some great overall advice that's good whether you're 50 or 70. It will help you lay the groundwork for a successful outcome and take some of the angst out of the process. The magic comes when you put together the puzzle pieces in a way that makes sense for you and your goals.

JOB-HUNTING TOOLS

There's a lot of ground to cover, and you will probably find yourself cherry-picking those elements that pertain to where you are in that journey. You might be just mulling the idea of finding a new job, or already hot on the hunt, or seeking part-time work to strengthen your retirement.

Let's dig into how you can begin scrutinizing your singular job-hunting tools—your résumé, your online persona and presence, your network, and so on.

First, write a short pitch, roughly one that takes 30 seconds to say, about the kind of job you're seeking and share it with friends, relatives, former colleagues, and really anyone else you can think of. This is your basic elevator pitch. It's great to have it memorized, so it pops out of your mouth when you meet someone who might be helpful. At that length, it's also easy to copy and paste into an email. Always ask if they know anyone you can talk to.

Second, you will be judged on your cover, so invest in an updated wardrobe, glasses (if you wear them), and a good haircut. Being physically in shape does make a difference.

I know these are window-dressing suggestions and really have nothing to do with what makes you a great candidate for a job. But it's the nature of the beast. Even on virtual interviews, this will deliver a subliminal message about who you are and your attitude. I personally feel more confident when I look the best I can, and you will too. And that energy and poise translates to the person you are talking to. It's infectious and powerful.

Do Your Research

Take the time to be certain that you're in synch with the technology and have the skills or certifications that are prerequisites for the job you're applying for. Have a working knowledge of what the trends are in your field or industry overall. This is a deeper part of your preparation, but the sooner you start the better.

One way to do that is to read through LinkedIn profiles of people that have the job that you're applying for. What do they say their skills are?

What happens when you don't have one of the "qualifications" needed for the job? Fuller gave me this example: Say, you're a human resource professional, and the job posting says you need to have experience with Workday, a rapidly growing resource management system many companies use today. If you don't have that experience, see if you can get qualified by taking an online course or a course at a community college. Another option is to find a temporary position through a company like Manpower or Adecco where you can get experience using the software.

To get a bead on the most relevant topics facing your industry and possible future employers, reach out to colleagues in your field to discuss which podcasts they're listening to or books and articles they've read lately. Having this knowledge will show that you're enthusiastically engaged in the latest news and developments in your field when you're doing interviews or networking.

Nitty-gritty knowledge will give you a leg up in interviews, but it also provides an inner coolness, or sense of security, that calmly centers you. You realize that you *are* qualified and prepared for the challenges faced by your potential employer and the broader industry. You're not living in the past. You get it. You look ahead out of curiosity—not fear.

That is a source of power. Knowledge turns to gusto and curiosity—both enormously helpful attributes when it comes to batting back ageist concerns and capturing a hiring manager's attention.

Be practical. "A lot of job seekers are looking for a job that's equal to, or greater than one they used to have," Fuller, who also cochairs the Harvard Business School Project on Managing the Future of Work, told me when I interviewed him for my Next Avenue column.

But that's a tough bill to fill. A widening training gap may dash that dream.

"The rapid pace of change in many occupations, driven in large part by advancing technologies, has made it extremely difficult for workers to obtain relevant skills," according to the Harvard report. "The evolution in job content has outstripped the capacity of traditional skills providers, such as education systems and other workforce intermediaries, to adapt. The perverse consequence is that developing the capabilities employers seek increasingly requires the candidate to be employed."[3]

"If you've been out of work for many months because your employer closed down, because you wanted to step away from the workplace out of concerns about health and Covid, because you got laid off because of Covid—whatever it is, you might have a very big gap in skills now," Fuller said. "Take a deep breath and be realistic about it because the easiest way to get that job you actually want today is to have a job."

For an in-depth source of help, AARP offers AARP Skills Builder for Work (aarp.org/workskills), an online platform to help older workers get necessary skills to get hired.

RETURNSHIPS

Older workers who have been away from the workplace for an extended time and are seeking a job face special challenges. There are programs and resources to help.

Goldman Sachs, for example, offers a "returnship" to give previously employed professionals who have been out of the workforce for two or more years an opportunity to restart their careers. The returnship is a paid 12-week program.

In partnership with reacHIRE,[4] Schneider Electric's Return-to-Work program is designed for experienced professionals looking to return to the workforce following a career break of more than two years. This six-month full-time, paid program includes opportunities in sales, commercial operations, project management, and quality/data analytics. During the program, participants gain relevant work skills and experiences through projects and training. They also receive coaching as well as interview and résumé preparation. At the end of the program, participants may be eligible for full-time or extended contracting work at Schneider Electric, but it's not guaranteed.

Here are three other good programs for workers 50+ who want to return to work:

- **iRelaunch** (irelaunch.com). This site is the leading source of information for getting back to work. It produces the iRelaunch Return to Work Conferences and has worked with more than 200 global companies on return-to-work initiatives of all kinds, through which thousands of relaunchers have restarted careers.

- **OnRamp Fellowship** (onrampfellowship.com). The fellowship pairs experienced lawyers returning to the workforce after a career interruption with law firms and legal departments in the United States for yearlong paid positions.

- **Path Forward** (pathforward.org/). Path Forward is a nonprofit organization that helps people restart their careers after time spent focused on caregiving. The specialty: working with companies to create and run midcareer internships—also known as "returnships"—that give professionals a jump start back to their careers.

The idea is to not get stuck in a conviction that you must have a specific job. Open your search up to a position that's close to what you want to get back in the swing. "If you get to 80 percent of what you're looking for, be very, very careful about putting it aside in the quest for a 100 percent, particularly if you've been out of the workforce for more than a few months," Fuller advised.

Develop an Online Identity

Create a solid online identity. I recommend having a Facebook, Twitter, and, especially, a LinkedIn profile. LinkedIn for most white-collar workers is your personal flyer to present yourself to everyone from hiring managers to people you'd like to meet for informational interviews.

Make sure you include awards you've won, YouTube videos of speeches you've done, PowerPoint presentations, and maybe even a video résumé. Upload a photo that shows you smiling, or at least looking approachable. Use a headline that runs below your name that says what you do, your expertise.

"Don't write: 'I'm seeking new opportunities' under your picture," Steve Dalton from Duke University's Fuqua School of Business career center suggested when I asked his advice on this topic. "I think it makes it seem like an advertisement and smacks of being somewhat needy. Instead use one- or two-word descriptors in your LinkedIn profile, each followed by a vertical slash. Some examples are: problem solver/team builder/mentor/. I like it because it's constructive and it's positive." Profiles of other professionals in your field can give you ideas.

Your "about" statement should be written in your voice, using *I*, as if you are telling a new colleague or acquaintance about your work. For instance, you might explain one of your proudest accomplishments and what you relish most about the work you do. Show off your personality here. Think conversational banter.

The beauty of your profile is that an employer can find succinct information about you and your experience in a straightforward format that quickly shows where you work or have worked, how long you were there, what job titles you've held, where you studied, and even other people you're connected to that the employer might know as well.

Do a LinkedIn search to discover people you know at firms where you're looking for opportunities. Follow leaders in your field. Look at the profiles of people in your industry and desired position to get ideas on how you might tweak your own.

And instead of eyeing LinkedIn as a place where you can ask someone to help you in some way, look at ways to lift someone else. "Liking" or sharing articles you see posted are two great ways to build goodwill. Congratulate someone on a promotion or a new job, or comment positively on something they have published or achieved. Ultimately, that karma will come back your way.

Search for people you know who work at firms where you might want to apply, or you know are hiring, and send an invitation to connect.

The LinkedIn job board is top-drawer. You set the parameters for what you're after in terms of time commitment, location, and duties. Sign up to have new job listing alerts sent to you and apply straight from the site. And let recruiters know you are open for work. If you are currently employed, however, you should skip that.

You can also easily search the name of an employer on the site and find the closest connection you have to someone who works there. If it's someone who shares an alumni relationship with you, even better.

Invisibility is a problem in today's job hunt. You should be moderately active and engaged on these social media sites—but keep politics out of it. These public-facing sites are for you to showcase your talent and accomplishments mixed with supporting others and some fun stuff, too, but nothing off-color, mind you.

Clean up any random posts, pictures, or tags from other people on your Facebook page, Twitter account, and any other social media site you would prefer a potential employer not see. Some of this might already be done with privacy settings, but not always.

And don't be afraid to ask for help if you're comfortable with the virtual public forum. One posting from a 50+ former colleague caught my attention:

> Hello, everyone. After a series of unforeseen events, I find myself unemployed. I would so appreciate any help you could give

in terms of contacts with people you know, job openings, or free-lance opportunities. I am looking mainly in the areas of editing/writing/communications in the marketing, healthcare, and publishing fields. Law firms are a particular interest. Also, please check out my new website!

Thanks so much, friends.

Within hours, she had 100 of her "friends" comment, offer to help, and promise to connect with a private message.

Google yourself to discover what's out there about you. See what pops up in the first few pages of your search. There might even be someone with your same name with a checkered background who could be confused with you—be prepared to explain that if it comes up in an interview.

I tell you this with all seriousness because a hiring manager, and probably anyone who is interviewing you, will do a Google search to find out more about you. They are particularly looking for clues to who you are outside of the workplace, your hobbies, your passions, and so on. But also, they want to know who you know that they know. Do you share friends or business contacts?

For many employers, it's not only about the candidate with the best credentials; it's about who's the best fit overall for the team. Are you likeable and interesting? Do you have a sense of humor and playfulness? Are there points of connection they can make with you via shared activities you both enjoy, causes or charities you support, or even places you've lived or traveled? Perhaps you have an adorable Labrador retriever just like they do. This visibility is where your broad personal and business colleague networks built over decades play in your favor over a younger candidate.

Update Your Résumé

It's important to have a current résumé on hand so you can quickly reply to unexpected openings. (See my story below.) Keep it brief—no more than two pages. Present an organized snapshot of employers and job titles with your challenge, action, and result (CAR) stories.

Remove "Responsible for . . ." in your résumé. These are mind-numbing descriptions. Instead tell an accomplishment story that screams results. For example, short extracts such as you slashed costs by 20 percent, increased revenues by 25 percent, or delivered a project two months ahead of schedule. Make each bullet under your experience an achievement, with a number (a dollar figure or percentage). Your capability to make an impact that can be *measured* is what separates you from other candidates.

Think advertisement, not obituary. Most recruiters will scan it in 20 or 30 seconds. Choose a traditional font, such as Times New Roman, in 9- to 12-point size, and use black type on white paper. Other fonts to consider are Arial, Calibri, Cambria, and Tahoma.

Stick to the most recent 10 to 15 years of experience. Avoid giving dates when it comes to decades-old experience—and only include jobs if they're pertinent to the work you're currently seeking. There's no need for college graduation dates.

Never include your "objective" in your résumé. Honestly, no one cares. It's their objective that matters.

It bears repeating because it happens all the time—your résumé and any correspondence with a hiring manager or potential employer must be error-free. Microsoft Word can help you spot typos and some grammar issues. Grammarly and VMock are free online tools that can serve as another set of virtual eyes. VMock can show if you've repeated action words and will offer substitutes.

CUSTOMIZATION IS VITAL

Too many job seekers use the same résumé for every position. It's imperative that you match the experience and skills you cite in your résumé with the exact skills employers say they're seeking in their job postings. This means you will have a basic résumé saved and then customize it to suit each application. For example, if you're applying for a sales manager position, emphasize your leadership qualifications. If you're applying to a high-paying sales position with no direct reports, stress your sales skills and ability to operate independently.

Remember, your résumé is rarely seen by a human being in the initial evaluation. You are writing something that will be scanned and assessed by an artificial intelligence (AI) system looking for ways to slash the pile of applicants.

Fuller believes that many older workers applying for jobs lose track of this fact. "They're writing something that is going to be assessed by a not very smart AI system that is looking for reasons to winnow down the pile of applicants," he said. "An applicant wants to very carefully study the job description offered."

A large majority (88 percent) of employers told the Harvard researchers that qualified candidates with high skills are vetted out of the process because they do not match the exact criteria established by the job description. That number rose to 94 percent in the case of workers with middle skills.

In my job as a writer, I'd be foolish to just lift entire phrases out of somebody else's writing. That's called plagiarism and a fireable offense. But that's exactly what employers want you to do.

"If your last job description was program director, but in this company that you're applying to, it seems to be called project manager, call yourself a project manager. Use the exact phrases that the job description does," Fuller advised. "Don't add value. Just take the phrase that's used and plug it in, assuming you're not lying."

There are keyword scanners that can help. For example, Jobscan .co is a free service that lets you upload your résumé and add a job description. It will then help you tailor the résumé.

For overall résumé help, AARP Resume Advisor offers an expert review gratis. LinkedIn has a search feature that can help you find a résumé writer (linkedin.com/services/l2/resume-writers) who can assist you. Receive free quotes from potential writers via the site's matchmaking service after you fill in a short form describing your needs, such as whether you are looking for help with a traditional résumé or your LinkedIn profile.

A few professional résumé services include: AvidCareerist (avid careerist.com), Career Trend (careertrend.net), Chameleon Résumés (chameleonrésumés.com), Executive Career Brand (executive careerbrand.com), and Great Résumés Fast (greatrésumésfast.com). You can also find certified résumé writers through Career Directors International (careerdirectors.com) or the National Resume Writers Association (thenrwa.com). Fees range from $300 to $1,500 or more.

Update your email address if you're still working with an AOL or Hotmail address. Those instantly date you. Gmail is easy to set up and free. Outlook is another option. Or if you have your own website, you can go with an email address like mine, kerry@kerryhannon.com.

Create a Personal Website

Depending on your background, your expertise, and the type of work opportunity you are pursuing, a personal website can be a great way to market yourself, especially if you plan to make contract work your *full-time* work. It will help boost your business by showing you as a trusted expert in your field.

You can launch a single-page website with a professional photo and a colorful description of your career experience, expertise, and interests—basically, you're using the site to create a highlighted résumé.

Your personal website is also where you can display testimonials from happy clients, attach videos of you speaking on various topics, and post blogs you've written that reveal your know-how and more.

Add new content frequently. Regular blog posts will boost your site's ranking with search engines like Google Chrome and Safari when potential clients are looking for you.

If you need something more involved, you can always hire a freelance web designer to set it up for you. That's what I did. You can search for one on Fiverr, LinkedIn ProFinder, Upwork, or TaskRabbit, for example, or ask around your circle of friends and family for a referral. I found my webmaster years ago via a landscaper working on my yard—his wife. It's not expensive to set one up, and there are many affordable hosts out there, including DreamHost, FatCow, GoDaddy, Hostinger, Hostwinds, and Wix.

BUILD YOUR CONFIDENCE

After you've been out of work for a while, you can forget your worth. You take for granted your accomplishments and contributions, and, as a result, you dismiss what makes you spark and stand out in a field of applicants.

Extract the words to authentically sell yourself. Ask people close to you professionally and personally, whose judgments you value, to send you a note telling you briefly what they believe are your best skills and talents, your personality, and the responsibilities that you excel at. You may have already done this as you prepared for your job search. If not, get to it.

Pull out your performance reviews from previous employers. Make a bulleted list of achievements that pop out. You've probably forgotten some of them. Put that list in front of you during any kind of virtual or phone interview. It can quell your nerves because you're not thinking off the top of your head when a recruiter or hiring manager asks about your past challenges and how you solved them.

Keep track of positive comments others make about you and your work as you move along through your job search—and, hey, your entire life. "You're reliable, tenacious, trustworthy." Or, "You quickly resolve problems."

I keep a computer folder filled with the positive affirmations and testimonials that others—from readers to listeners to colleagues and clients—send me about my work. When I feel lost, I pull those testimonials out and give myself permission to accept them as my truth. Allow yourself to absorb how those around you value what you do and who you are.

All these things will come in handy whether you're in an interview, an informational conversation, or networking. Now you have the words to describe yourself that I admit can be hard to spit out if you're humble or reticent to brag on yourself.

MY MOST RECENT JOB
SEARCH EXPERIENCE

Here's what happened to me. It was in the months leading up to the pandemic, but the lessons I learned are applicable to you right now.

I wasn't looking for an in-house job. I've run my own one-woman media business for more than two decades. In fact, I still scratch my head about what I was thinking when this came along. But I must admit, it was partially because I was feeling burned out and yearning for a steady, reliable paycheck and someone to pay my $800 a month health insurance bill. Here's the story.

A colleague told me about an interesting opportunity to lead a new initiative for a global publishing company. I was intrigued. It offered an audacious challenge and a large platform and involved making a difference in a business arena that was part of my personal mission—boosting small business operators and entrepreneurs—the soul of our economy.

The primary mantra I tell everyone about job hunting is it is *never* about you, it's about them, the employer, and what you can do to make them successful, not you. You will discover below what I mean by this.

Here is how it all unfolded and my top blunders.

I hadn't created a résumé since I applied for my last in-house position at *USA Today* decades ago. I suggested that the prospective employer, who was interested in meeting with me about the position (after my contact at the firm connected us) look at my LinkedIn profile to get a snapshot of my experience. To me, that says it all, period, and it should be obvious that I was qualified.

Unfortunately, since it was a large employer, they have a certain way of doing things. The job had been posted through the HR department and they needed a résumé that would glide through an electronic submission process. And, of course, I needed to match the keywords in that job posting to the contents of my résumé.

While the hiring manager was eager to talk, the rules must be followed. I groaned. I didn't even have a good template to use that showcased my decades of experience. I emailed my then 28-year-old niece, Caitlin Bonney, who had just landed an amazing job after graduating from her master's program, and asked her to send me her résumé to use as my model.

I scanned the employer's job posting to embed the keywords—*conceive, develop, deliver, enhance*—in the snapshots of my previous positions and accomplishments and included my CAR (challenges, actions, and results) stories to highlight my ability to build an audience and produce successful events.

I chose a traditional font, 12-point Times New Roman, and used black type on a white background. I stuck to the most recent 10 to 15 years of experience, avoided giving dates, and only included jobs that were relevant to the work at hand.

I asked my sister to help me chop it down to one-and-a-half pages. (She is super good at this kind of thing.) I read it aloud several times. I was pleased with the result. My résumé told a story, rather than just providing a list of job titles and dates. I was proud of it.

But it was time-consuming. And in full disclosure, while I understood the protocol, simmering beneath the surface was resentment at having to fine-tune a résumé at this stage of my working life. They already knew who I was.

Ego check, Kerry!

Even though I hadn't gone on a job interview for eons, I brought my A game to the meeting. I was confident and relaxed and full of ideas. Generating ideas is one of the things I do best. I love the creative challenge. My eyes shine. I start to talk fast. I feel the energy bouncing off me.

But in retrospect, I could have done better. Here's why: Although the two people interviewing me over lunch were not much younger than me, I did spend a little more time than I should have talking about work experiences from days gone by and reminiscing since I did have some previous business connections with one of them. (I was even good friends with one of my interviewer's ex-girlfriends. I didn't bring her up! But we both knew this.)

But the worst thing I did was rattle on about why their job description was faulty in some way or unrealistic, even. And it was. *I* knew what they really needed. To be fair, they didn't have any idea about what they wanted from the newly created position, so they threw in the whole kitchen sink. It was a job for several people, not just one superwoman.

No one seemed flummoxed by my comments, at least on the surface. In review, I should have known better than to let loose from my lofty perch with my professional advice on how they should write a job description and what they truly needed from someone in the position to accomplish.

Hubris, anyone?

My performance didn't kick me out of contention. In fact, they asked me to send them a "blueprint" proposal for how I would approach the new initiative on several levels. I spent hours and hours on this task. I gave it a detailed assessment, showing off how smart I was and what clever ideas I would bring to the organization's effort.

It pained me to give away my expertise for *free*. I knew it was wrong. I should have passed on this step and walked away immediately. By then, though, I was too invested in the process and I wanted to see it through to the end. My self-esteem kicked in and I fought back my gut response to pull myself out of the process. The powers that be gushed in response to my outline. They called it an "impressive document," effusively thanked me, and told me how much they loved it.

The final interview was on the phone. This was my fifth or sixth conversation with the hiring team, which included the top executive in charge (I had lost track and each interview gobbled an hour or so of my time, plus my prep work). It seemed to be going well, but during the discussion, my interviewer made a passing remark about how there was so much about me in my proposal and what I would do to accomplish their goals. He felt I wasn't paying enough homage to the company's existing brand and resources.

Aha! I had let my ego get in the way yet again. And truth be told, when I reread it and reconstructed all the in-person and phone interviews in my head, I had done quite a bit of bragging all along the way. This is a danger zone for experienced workers because we're challenged with selling ourselves in job interviews, but there is a fine, unwritten line you shouldn't cross.

Jeepers. I dove straight into that trap with gusto.

For the right job, compromise is key, and relocation may be a necessity, even in the new world of remote work. I wasn't playing. I knew this was a possibility when I sent my résumé, but I didn't think it applied to me. I was "special." After nearly 30 years of living in Washington, DC, the thought of moving to the New York City area, where this employer was based, wasn't on my dream list. I had already done all of that back in my 20s.

I was certain that I would be an exception, of course, that I would be working remotely with in-office meetings on a regular schedule. It would be copasetic. After all, I was a proven, disciplined remote worker, and the position would require a lot of travel, which I was game to do. Requiring face time in an office and daily elevator meetups for synergy seemed old-fashioned and quaint, to stay the least.

Wrong! They wanted all of that. The hiring manager said that it was possible, in time, that I could work half-time in my home office, but the travel to and from headquarters—the transportation and hotel bills—would come out of my pocket. I couldn't imagine doing that.

Moreover, I wasn't honest about one huge stumbling block from the start.

The job didn't fit my mission. To explain this disconnect isn't easy—even now. In essence, the employer was looking to build out a new splashy platform that would generate revenue and showcase the publisher's brand in a grand marketing move. In contrast, my vision was about the audience they wished to serve. I wanted to provide a platform to lift people up and help them to succeed through advice, a supportive community, and affordable resources.

As Simon Sinek (simonsinek.com), author of *Start with Why?* so eloquently preaches: I do know my *why*. My *why* is making a positive difference in people's lives. This employer's *why* was making money from those people.

Mic drop. Disconnect.

In the end, they hired a woman two decades younger than me who lived within commuting distance to the headquarters.

Lesson learned.

6

Showtime

This is where the rubber meets the road, as the saying goes. Yep—it's boogie-woogie time.

Start with the no-strings-attached interviews. Informational interviews can be an important way to develop your network and center your job search. In the spirit of multigenerational collaboration, for some insight, I asked my go-to niece, Caitlin, who was a pro at these when she was looking for her first big job after graduate school at Duke University's Nicholas School of the Environment. Now, she regularly mentors graduating students to help them navigate their careers.

INFORMATIONAL INTERVIEW TIPS

I was taken with Caitlin's counsel and want to share it with you. It works for job seekers our age too. First, if someone agrees to talk to you, make sure you know as much as you can about their life and career, she said. Ask via an email when is the best time and what platform the person prefers to use to talk. Then never wait or hesitate once they give you the nod. Take the lead to set the meeting up. Send a calendar invite with a Zoom link (or platform of their choice). And share with them your LinkedIn profile and basic résumé.

Here are some guidelines for your conversation:

Twenty minutes is plenty of time for these kinds of chats. Up front let them know what your ask is—for example, their ideas about what jobs and industries your skills and experience might suit.

Explain what you're looking for in a new position. You may have already done this in your initial outreach, but it will help them frame what they share with you. What drives you? Tell a story from your life that sums that up. Be honest, and tell them you hope they can help you get a foot in the door down the road at that person's firm or with someone they know. No reason to dance around that desire. Full transparency.

Have a list of questions handy. What attracted them to the industry? What has helped them succeed in their career? You want to *learn* about them and their jobs. What do they see as the areas with the most opportunities right now? What skills are in demand? Who else should you talk to about career paths and opportunities in the field? Remember, you're trying to bond with another person, to make a human connection, so be enthusiastic and confident and *enjoy* the conversation.

Afterward, promptly send an email note of thanks. Express your appreciation for their time and state something that you learned or that was memorable. If you invite them to connect on LinkedIn, be sure to send a personalized message with a reference to your conversation. If applicable, follow up with a job posting for their company and ask whether you might be a good fit.

In addition to this advice, narrow the list of people you want to contact to only those at companies where you would like to work, or those you respect as leaders or visionaries. Those are the typical categories these informational interviews fall into, and they help to identify who to seek out.

Some of these will be long shots, so accept that and move to the next one if you don't get a response. But give it at least two emails before you let it go—it's good to be a little tenacious here. People are busy. I get so many emails some days, that it's easy to lose track of them. It's usually best to mention how you are connected to the person or why you selected them to try to talk to for advice. Flattery can help in either case. Mention that you admire their work, or have heard amazing things about them from a mutual friend or colleague.

Stay out of the conversation as much as you can once you tee it up. When we're in job-hunting mode, we're hardwired to put on the razzmatazz of selling why we would be a great hire for an organization.

People will have a great and perhaps better lingering impression of you, even if they don't realize it consciously, if you can show that you're sincerely zealous about what *they* do and their career path.

You're not asking them to hire you, you're asking them to share their insight. Who doesn't like to do that?

DEVELOP A SUPPORT GROUP

Connect with other job seekers you might know. An informal meetup on a regular basis can help you support each other and be accountable to staying on the path to finding a new position. You might even hear of jobs that aren't right for you but could be perfect for one of your search partners.

With a job support group, you can let off steam and vent—a huge stress buster. And you might not appreciate it, but you benefit by helping others through brainstorming with them, acting as a sounding board, and connecting them to your network.

It feels good. You're contributing and your advice and help is valued by someone else. It goes both ways. Some days you're the giver. Others the receiver. An added upside to being part of a support group is that you have regular meetings. These keep you on track in a tangible fashion. That day, that time, is all about job hunting, and you are forced to stop procrastinating and focus on your search.

Friends and family care and want to help, but they will tire of asking you how it's going, and you will resent having to respond while the search continues.

"It's often awkward," Ofer Sharone, associate professor of sociology at the University of Massachusetts Amherst, told me. "Friends don't quite know what to say and they may distance themselves, or friends might ask too many questions that suggest the job seekers are doing something wrong."

The support that comes from bringing people together in a job search group who are in the same boat sends the message that there's nothing wrong with you.

"Rather there's something wrong with the way hiring is happening," Sharone said. "They can see in the group that there are other people in the room who are very qualified, very skilled. That's essential for the resilience it takes to keep searching."

That's the human side of a job search. Don't take this lightly. This is where the surprising can happen, the unexpected connection, the unforeseen opportunity.

There are so many virtual tools like one-way job interviews where you aren't even interviewed by a person but by a computer program.

The more automated the job market becomes, the more valuable it is to have a human being advocating for you.

REFERRALS GET RESULTS

The adage "it's not what you know, it's who you know" takes on a whole new level of meaning in today's job hunt marketplace. My research has shown that up to 70 percent of all jobs are not published on publicly available job search sites, and anywhere from 50 percent to as much as 80 percent of jobs are filled through networking. One of my favorite networking success stories to illustrate this comes from Keith Cooper, the salesman you met in Chapter 4 who found work as a project manager. He has since been promoted several times. It was while he was out sailing in Florida that he met his future boss who just happened to have a job opening to fill in New Jersey.

Most full-time positions are either filled internally or through referrals. Employers fancy hiring people they know either directly or indirectly. It is less risky. And the perception by hiring managers that someone will be a good fit ramps up substantially when an insider gives them a nod.

I can't emphasize this enough—employee referrals are the chief source of hires—not applications for online job postings. Employers love it when someone who already works for the company can testify to a person's character and competence. And the employee making the reference may even get something too. Many employers offer a referral bonus if someone is hired and performs well for a couple of months.

USING JOB BOARDS EFFECTIVELY

Does this mean that zapping an application for a job opening you spy on a job board is for naught? Of course not. You never know. And plenty of folks get wonderful jobs this way, but it is a long shot for most applicants over age 50.

Please don't be depressed or lose faith if you never hear a peep. That's depressingly common as we have already reviewed. It's that insider track and network that is going to be your best way to get anyone to pay attention to you.

At this point, I have probably put a target on my back from the job board operators out there, many of whom I know and value. And yes, as I just said, jobs can come through for you via this route, but having someone you know at that firm (or someone who knows someone) where you applied and who can then follow up for you will be hugely helpful. You've got to make that personal connection in today's workplace. That's how you stand out and bust through the automatic tracking systems.

Even if you might not actually score a job through one of these virtual job boards, they are a great tool for learning what jobs are out there now, what companies are hiring, and the qualifications required. A company's career section where jobs are posted is potentially a better avenue than the broader job board sites like Indeed.com. An association affiliated with your field is another job board source. And if you have a specialty, look for niche job boards specifically for that profession. In my case, journalismjobs.com is one.

LinkedIn offers a few ways to hear about professional postings. The basic one is the jobs button at the top of the screen. You can search for jobs by a slew of filters from company type to, say, full-time or contract jobs. You can also search by job title, salary, benefits, skills, or location. You can screen by remote, hybrid, or on-site positions.

And you can set alerts to let you know when jobs that match your criteria are posted. You can also apply directly from LinkedIn using your profile and track the status of the application. Importantly, you can check a box to let recruiters know you're open to work, which is only visible to recruiters. You have the option, though, to allow all LinkedIn members to see your availability.

As you look at online job postings, keep an open mind. It's easy to get sucked into trying to replicate your old job, as Harvard's Joseph Fuller discussed. The truth is you can do so many things.

Here's what happens to me when I look at job postings in my field, and I suspect it will be the same for you. Either I have a knee-jerk reaction that it's a retread to something I was doing a decade or more ago, or maybe the employer is asking for so many duties and responsibilities and qualifications, that you just say . . . huh? (Recall the job interview I described in Chapter 5?)

I regularly get turned off by the sheer litany of requirements—exhausting to read through, let alone to apply for. Then the kicker is they generally say something like 8 to 10 years of related experience. Ahem . . . I have nearly 30. I suspect many of you have experienced this firsthand.

It Isn't Always About Pay

Meantime, when you get to a stage in a job search process where salary is discussed, the pay might seem ridiculously low, given all the experience you bring to the position. I get this all the time with freelance writing gigs that pay by the word. It's tough not to feel resentful and undervalued. But in a full-time position, there are ways you can eventually discuss more flextime, vacation days, and other perks that can make it work. Research what the job pays on average, if you can, via sites like Salary.com, Payscale.com, and Glassdoor.com. The Bureau of Labor Statistics' Occupational Handbook also lists median salaries and ranges for a plethora of positions.

It isn't always about the pay when it comes to succeeding in the new workplace. I heard this example from Andy Levine, who runs the Second Act Stories Podcast (Secondactstories.org).

Dave Lazarus worked for 35 years in information technology and software development and programming. But at 60, he lost his job. Faced with what he felt might be a tough slog trying to find another IT job, he found a job teaching chess to elementary school students, first in an after-school program in Short Hills, New Jersey, and then as a private teacher. It was his passion since he was a kid. "Chess is not an age thing, and these kids keep me on my toes," he said in his interview with Levine. "They are very sharp."

The popular Netflix series *The Queen's Gambit* led to a burst of demand for online chess lessons for students in grades 1 through 5 for Lazarus. "What's most rewarding is just to see the kid get it, and you go, '*Wow*.' I always tell people, I'd do it for free, but it's nice to get paid."

INTERVIEW PREP AND TACTICS

Notching an interview is the holy grail. Once you step onto the interview stage for a job, you catch a wind for sure. A twinge of excitement creeps in. Just getting the call or email to set up a time to talk can be a shot of adrenaline. You try to caution yourself not to get ahead of yourself, get your hopes up, or open yourself up for the pain if it doesn't lead to a job offer.

Ride with the wind for now. That hope will motivate you to really prepare. Don't sabotage your enthusiasm. Conversely, don't let down your guard and coast into the interview with the attitude that at last they recognize your experience and talent and you're on your way.

Nope, this is when you double down with your prep work on several levels, depending on the person you will be meeting with. Find as much out as possible about the person who will interview you and any current news at the company that's relevant or might come up in a conversation.

You want to be ready, but not overly so. Being too practiced can confine you from going with the flow. A great interview is a dance with improvisation and extemporaneity. In fact, I think it often helps to take an acting or improv class before you even begin a job search. Improv is all about building a conversation between two people in a positive way. Enroll in a public speaking course or join a Toastmasters Club (toastmasters.org) to hone your interview routine.

Focus on three conversation points that are most important for you to convey about why you are perfect for this job. If it's a live virtual interview, post sticky notes on your computer or on the walls in front of your camera to prompt you about the three key selling points. If a conversation gets rolling with a recruiter or hiring manager/ potential boss, whoever is trotted out to talk to you, these facts will help you stay focused. They will serve as an anchor for your conversation, while not scripting you with written-out answers that would make you sound stilted. With just three points, you can deftly pivot in new directions as the conversation unfolds organically.

Keep in mind that a job posting describes what is expected of someone, so subtly weaving some of those phrases into your interview conversation can help. It's a subconscious message in some ways.

For instance, one job I looked at in my field had these phrases:

Versatility will be key.

This will mean orchestrating a highly **collaborative** process.

A significant part of this role will include **coordinating** and editing the work of a growing team.

The mission is to give readers **honest, independent, and trustworthy advice** on a range of topics.

What You'll Do

- Ensure that content is **high-quality, accurate, and objective**
- **Manage a schedule,** cadence, and process for integrating input from a variety of stakeholders

What We're Looking For

- Top-notch writing and editing skills with **an eye for detail and nuance**
- **Commitment** to helping readers understand—and identify what is best for their particular needs
- Capacity for **working independently** and with minimal direction
- Ability to prioritize **and manage multiple deadlines** simultaneously
- **Experience with spreadsheets** and Asana is a plus

There was more, but the idea is to slip into an interview conversation some of this exact language, but ever so casually.

Importantly, prepare a handful of questions to ask your interviewer. Some of my favorites are: finding out what the person loves about his or her job, what attracted the person to the company, and what the biggest challenge will be for anyone who steps into the role you are interviewing for.

Give the job interviewer a story about yourself that he or she can identify with, as Duke's Dalton tells his Duke students.

"The way to overcome ageism is to give people a story that makes sense about why you want to work there," he said. "If you're over 50, there's probably a moment in your life where your current story starts . . . or that moment where you took a completely different path, wherever your hero story is."

This tactic helps people understand what motivates you because they get an appreciation for your most important personal experience. And never forget to slip in the word *curious* from time to time. That's a trigger that can leave an impression that you're eager to learn and try new things and embrace a changing workplace.

"If you just repeat what your responsibilities were and where you work or worked, you're just reading your résumé out to them, that's not adding any value, nor building any rapport," Dalton told me.

Show Respect

It's not unusual to find yourself in a situation where it feels like you're more qualified than the person who is interviewing you. Something shifts in your manner, your voice, your attitude. It can be subconscious. Watch out for overconfidence or arrogance creeping into your demeanor.

Show respect. They are in that job for a reason. Always remember to be true to yourself, honest, and forthright. Keep it conversational. Focus on the company's needs right now and in the future, and how you fit into that scheme to help both the employer and your potential future boss to succeed.

Prepare for Virtual Interviews

Make the most of virtual interviews. These ramped up during the pandemic and are here to stay. You'll want to be dressed as you would be if you were meeting in someone's office. Don't just dress the part, also bring the same energy and enthusiasm to the virtual interview that you would to an in-person interaction.

Make sure you're set up in a place where you're relaxed and it's free of distractions, so you can focus. You might use headphones for the best audio and to prevent any feedback or echoes. I find the microphone on my MacBook Air is perfectly fine, but you should test out what is best on your device. I also have a Snowball microphone and a lavalier one that I have used occasionally.

Check your camera view when you sign on to whatever platform they are using, say, Google Meet, Zoom, or GoToMeeting. Confirm that your face is well lit from the front. Pro tip: I use two desk lamps on the sides of my computer—one on each side of my laptop—and a ring light set behind my laptop's camera. As a reminder about where to look, place a sticky note next to your camera at the top and center of your screen. Prop your laptop up so that your eyes are level with the camera. I use a stack of books. Keep your eyes on that lens if you can, and listen.

For many of us, staring at a camera doesn't feel natural—because it isn't. Remember to smile and nod intermittently, as you would during an in-person conversation. And limit any distractions around you, so you're not tempted to look away from your computer screen or even look down at yourself on camera.

Skip the good-humored Zoom background of a beach or the Golden Gate Bridge. It's distracting. Plus, your actual office background can provide subliminal information about you and your personality that can work in your favor and help you stand out as a candidate, if you have taken the time to stage it.

SUGGEST A TEMPORARY ASSIGNMENT

If you sense a hiring manager is interested in giving you a job but waffling, consider asking whether it would be possible to hire you in as a consultant, contractor, or intern, so he or she can appraise you after several weeks.

In your job search, as well, be open to working these types of temporary engagements. Sometimes, they can lead to a full-time position.

For example, if you are a marketing manager or an editor, consider using platforms like Upwork that provide a marketplace for someone with skills to work as an independent consultant on a contingent or gig basis for potential employers.

"That's better than sitting in your house on the lake, in Maine, hoping to get a job," Joseph Fuller from Harvard Business School told me. "Similarly, a lot of companies use those jobs as rent-to-own jobs. Let me see what kind of job Joe does. He gets along well with everybody. I wonder if he would take this job full time."

The great benefit of these arrangements is they allow both you and the employer to check out each other with little risk. And they can also fill in gaps in your résumé between full-time gigs. There is more about apprenticeships, fellowships, and internships in terms of changing careers in a later chapter.

TARGET THE RIGHT
COMPANIES FOR YOU

Only send applications for jobs at companies where you would be delighted to work. Otherwise, it's a waste of time for everyone. I would pick the 10 that most appeal to you, or even go to the websites of 10 places you'd really like to work and cruise the job board to see what might fit.

Sally forth when you find one that's exciting. You never know how this will play out until you try. Write in the cover letter precisely what attracts you to this firm or nonprofit; explain why what they do resonates with you; and let them know who you know there who has told you great things about their experience working for them. These letters can be short, maybe three paragraphs. First, say what job you are applying for, making sure you describe the job exactly as advertised. Second, discuss why this job is the cat's pajamas and why you're the perfect candidate. Last, talk about any connection you might have to the company. End with "I'm eager to learn more" or something along those lines.

Check out companies that are hip to hiring older workers. To best set yourself up for success both when job hunting and once you're on the job, focus on employers who unequivocally embrace your experience.

For older workers, it's not enough to have a job, Doug Dickson told me. He is chair of the Encore Boston Network (encoreboston network.org), a community of individuals, policy makers, advisors, coaches, advocates, researchers, businesses, nonprofits, and government agencies dedicated to making it possible for people over 50 to do purposeful work. "We want to work where our experience is valued, where organizations want us, and where we will be given a chance to do what we do best," he explained.

Startups, small associations, colleges, and universities are often open to hiring an experienced worker who can don several hats and manage a range of duties.

If you have a company on your target list that you'd love to work for, reach out to people you know who work there right now, or did before they retired, and find out what you can about the culture. Do older workers get tapped for innovative projects? Are they part of the conversation? Are they getting promoted or made to feel welcome and integral to the success of the firm?

Sometimes you can find reviews on sites like Glassdoor.com that provide employee feedback on a range of employers. Even the images a firm displays on its website can give you an inkling to how older workers are viewed. If it's all youth and juice, this might not be the best place for you ultimately.

AARP is the big player in working to persuade employers to hire experienced workers, as it should be. "The idea is to engage with employers on the value of a multigenerational workforce and the impact of age diversity on the bottom line," Kara Cohen, AARP Massachusetts outreach manager, explained to me.

The AARP Employer Pledge: Experience Valued program (aarp .org/work/job-search/job-seeker) is a national initiative to direct job seekers to employers that value and are hiring experienced workers. Employers who sign the pledge agree that they:

- Recognize the value of experienced workers

- Believe in equal opportunity for all workers, regardless of age

- Recruit across diverse age groups

- Consider all applicants on an equal basis

More than 1,000 employers have signed the pledge, including AlliedBarton, Airbnb, American Red Cross, AT&T, Charles Schwab, Giant Eagle, H&R Block, Kimberly Clark, Manpower, National Institutes of Health (NIH), New York Life, Scripps Health, United Health Group, Walgreens, and Yellowstone National Park Lodges. For the full list, go to aarp.org/work/job-search/employer-pledge-companies.

AGE-FRIENDLY EMPLOYERS

The job board Retirementjobs.com is another leader in connecting employers with 50+ job seekers like us. I'm an admirer of what Tim Driver, president of the Age-Friendly Institute (institute.agefriendly.org/) and founder of RetirementJobs.com, has done. Driver has been pressing for age-friendly employers for years and has been steadily making inroads with the site. The aim is to identify and then vet employers to make sure it's all true what they say about being open and welcoming to older workers. Finally, the site honors the organizations with a certification as a Certified Age Friendly Employer (CAFE) that says they are committed to be a great place to work for older employees.

To earn the "age-friendly" designation, employers must meet criteria across a dozen categories from compensation to benefits to workplace culture. The team also reviews the top executives' commitment to hiring and retaining employees as well as creating an environment that is respectful of workers 50+. I was pleased to find that CAFE program participants include tech and creative firms, where age bias was once the most engrained. For a list of employers that have earned the Certified Age Friendly Employer designation, visit agefriendly.com/jobs.

Don't Overlook Nonprofits

If you really feel trapped in your job search, get out of your head and into the world. Volunteer your skill-based services at a nonprofit group. You can do this virtually or in person. It can be exactly the boost you need. The work keeps your résumé alive and your skills sharp. And, of course, you never know who you will meet there who might know of a job lead for you. A job might even grow from your volunteer work at that organization itself. You just never know. Plus, doing good works just makes you feel better about yourself.

Hiring managers consistently tell me that they view volunteer experience as comparable to formal work experience. Search for prospects at local nonprofits you already support. VolunteerMatch .org, HandsOnNetwork.org, and AARP's Giving Back are also good resources.

Seek out nonprofits that need your professional expertise at the Taproot Foundation and the Executive Service Corps. Bridgespan.org runs an online job board for nonprofit positions. Idealist.org has a searchable database of both volunteer and paid positions.

STAY OPEN TO POSSIBILITIES

A parting thought for 50+ job seekers whether you are looking to move up or over in your current organization or land a job with a new employer: At the heart of a job search strategy for workers over 50— when you see a job posting or hear about an opening, always push yourself to think imaginatively about how you can apply your skills in a new direction. In today's world having a clear view of how your skill set can shift outside of your comfort zone and outside of the field you have always worked in, will allow the space for doors to open and will give you the breathing room for possibilities to arise.

Remote Work

Remote work defines the new world of work. It was a global movement before the pandemic, but its acceptance and reality accelerated during the lockdown. The genie is out of the bottle and things are never going to go back to the way they once were.

Prior to the Covid-19 work-from-home mandates, workers of all ages had begun to request greater autonomy and flexibility in their work lives, and employers were slowly getting on board. In many cases, though, it was a manager-by-manager arrangement and a negotiated perk. Even if a company's top brass said they were all in on the benefits of a remote workforce and trusted their workers to get the job done like pros and on time, it was more lip service than actuality in many workplaces.

Today, companies of all sizes in a variety of businesses are running smoothly with workforces, in many cases, that are entirely remote. They've had to. Not all have embraced it, but they have learned management strategies and adopted policies to make it a win for all.

The financial upsides are clear. Employees no longer rack up commuting costs and miscellaneous workplace out-of-pocket expenses, including meals. Researchers at FlexJobs.com estimate that the average person can save around $4,000 a year by working from home.[1] And employers can lower office space rental tabs and other overhead.

One major caveat here: not all jobs have the luxury of letting you work from home. Some that don't include nurses and other healthcare workers, restaurant employees from cooks to waitstaff, truck drivers and delivery service personnel, assembly-line laborers, tradespeople from contractors to plumbers to tilers, and grocery-store stockers and checkout staff. They don't have the choice to work remotely if they want to stay employed. These aren't great pajama jobs. The truth is that while remote working has captured all the headlines since the pandemic began, working virtually is generally skewed toward white-collar positions.

The office, however, is not disappearing. A physical bricks-and-mortar workspace is an important hub for many businesses. It's the place where employees bond and are immersed in a company's culture. That camaraderie is core to building teams and retaining employees. And to be honest, when you're visible to the powers that be, the opportunities to be promoted and considered for new projects are more likely to come your way regardless of your age.

Employers know that minus those physical interactions and the relationships that can emerge from those connections on a regular basis, switching employers becomes easier to do for workers. Your job becomes more focused on salary and work that's engaging and challenging, rather than a gut attachment to a team, your office pals, and a certain company's mission or ethos. Divested of the hooks of relationships established and deepened in an office, jumping jobs is less encumbered and emotional.

"Without hallway conversations, chance encounters, and small talk over coffee, it's hard to feel connected even to my immediate team, much less build meaningful connections across the company," said Hannah McConnaughey, product marketing manager at Microsoft.[2]

Even with all the snazzy technology and easy-to-use videoconferencing, both employers and employees are wrestling with ways to energize workplace cultures and make employees, particularly new hires, feel like they are part of a larger team or mission when the virtual office is the primary work setting.

Hybrid workplaces that combine work-from-home and in-office time are one solution. But in some cases, this may lead to two work streams—remote and in-office—and that may pose a problem for advancement for those who opt for working remotely more so than their managers and colleagues.

THE MANY BENEFITS OF REMOTE WORK

I have found that many older workers have taken the shift to remote work in stride. The need for colleagues to kibbitz with is not nearly as important perhaps. Or you may just naturally know that having autonomy and control of your work environment simply makes you a happier and more engaged worker at this stage of your life. This is something I hear again and again.

Plus, the jobs many workers 50+ do are often suited to remote work. The Center for Retirement Research at Boston College calculates that 44 percent of workers age 55 to 64 and 47 percent of those 65 and older had jobs that can be done remotely.[3]

Some top remote job titles include accountant, customer service representative, project manager, recruiter, teacher, web developer, and writer. Other jobs that can be done remotely are bookkeepers, CFOs, controllers, administrative assistants, virtual assistants, medical transcriptionists, remote nurses, pharmacists, radiologists, and data entry.

Remote work can also help sideline ageism. Gotta love that! When your performance and productivity are what set you apart, and you're not subliminally judged by the gray in your hair or wrinkles on your neck, it can make a huge difference in all aspects of your working life, from your hiring attractiveness to getting promoted to being offered new opportunities by your employer. I know no one utters that sentiment aloud, but it's embedded in our work culture and has been for decades. Remote work can subtly circumvent that reality.

FEELING LEFT OUT

A friend of mine who works in a senior position for the federal government told me that a hard part for her working in her office is the clique-like behavior of younger colleagues. She's 55. They freeze her out, even if it's not intentional. And, in fact, she doesn't think it is. But they bond over impromptu bantering back and forth about culture topics.

When she does try to join in, it's awkward. They speed along in half sentences about things she has never heard of from the hip new bands to streaming shows, and even brands of sneakers. They're on the same wavelength, and it makes her feel out of step and an outsider.

It's that raw feeling of being left out, not in with the cool crowd, or the one who isn't picked for the team. Even at her level, it stings emotionally. It makes her mad that she feels that way, but it's a form of ageist behavior that is honestly not very subtle in the workplace today. It's like a plexiglass wall you can see through, but cannot break through. When she was remote, there was none of that feeling, and it was a relief.

Meantime, if mobility and health issues are an impediment to commuting into an office, or even working in the office itself, virtual offices can be a bonanza. Many workers say a health problem or disability had motivated the decision to step out of the workplace.

Then too, a remote job opens the possibility of moving to a town where the cost of living is lower or to be closer to family or friends, making working beyond your 60s, in some measure, even more appealing and doable.

The ability to work remotely vastly expands potential employers. If the job market for what you do is weak in your geographic area, the possibilities of where you can work virtually opens the door to employer possibilities around the globe.

According to an evaluation by FlexJobs.com, the top four reasons people seek remote work are: work-life balance, family, time savings, and easing commute stress.[4] But, of course, there are other factors too. One that comes to mind is that it can allow you to steer clear of office politics and distractions.

Another advantage to remote work is, if you're owned by a dog (or a cat), you have the pleasure of their company while you work. Can you say, stress buster? If it's a dog, you also have the advantage that comes from pushing back from the screen and taking your pooch for a walk and some fresh air—both huge psychological and physical boosts during a workday. This is a major lift for me, and I often connect with another remote worker in my neighborhood to get a dose of humanity, as well.

Finally, if you have caregiving duties for a child or an aging relative or parent, as I have had, you can often flex your work time around those responsibilities.

THE OUT-OF-SIGHT, OUT-OF-MIND PROBLEM

The drawback to remote work, though, is that for many women who are juggling the demands of remote work and caregiving, being out of sight, out of mind can be another barrier when it comes to promotions and pay raises. When you aren't schmoozing front and center with your manager or boss, it can be yet another concern women must deal with and magnifies the pay inequity issues that already exist in the workplace.

You can combat this. It comes down to consistent communication with your boss and tooting your own horn unabashedly to make sure your accomplishments are noted and celebrated—even very small ones. You can get lost in the office dynamic simply because you aren't present. I can't sugarcoat the reality of that stumbling block. So, if it's possible, do try to attend in-person gatherings or meetings on a regular basis if your employer provides those types of interactions. At the very least, never dismiss the importance of staying present in your manager's mind for all the good work you are doing and can do.

If it's not embarrassingly obvious by now, I love remote work. To be fair, when I was younger, I truly did relish having office pals and building deep friendships that have lasted a lifetime. And I know I was promoted and received great opportunities in some cases because I was visible to my bosses. Even then, though, I yearned for the flexibility to write from home, or to skip the office scene periodically. I wanted my bosses to give me freer rein than they could, or would, in those days. They never did. Sigh. I had to start my own business to become a remote worker. And to be truthful, I have never worked more hours in my life and never been happier.

FINDING A REMOTE JOB

Sharon Emek, founder of Work At Home Vintage Experts (WAHVE .com), a site for professionals over 50 who work from home for more than 300 insurance and accounting firms, was an innovator on the remote job front for older workers. She launched her service in 2010. Emek recognized that workers in this age cohort were eager to get out of the office but stay on the job.

She also saw the demand from employers to hire those who can step into the job with little training.

"We help retiring professionals continue their careers into retirement with work-from-home opportunities without sacrificing their work-life balance," Emek told me. "We also believe that businesses should have access to the most knowledgeable, highly capable professionals available at an affordable price."

Emek's site researches and vets employers for you, if those are the kinds of jobs you are seeking. There are other great sites that list openings at remote-friendly employers. See below for some of my top suggestions.

Keep in mind, though, that even with the pedal to the metal acceptance of remote working jobs, many remote listings are for temporary contract, freelance, or project-specific work that does not offer benefits. These opportunities can, however, lead to full-time employment eventually if all goes well. To get started, check out the FlexJobs.com annual list of employers that post the most remote job openings.

The big job boards, such as AARP's job board (jobs.aarp.org), CareerBuilder.com, Glassdoor.com, Indeed.com, and Monster.com are searchable for remote positions. Type "remote" in the search box that asks for what job title you are looking for. There are also several job boards dedicated to remote jobs. In addition to Flexjobs.com, here are some of my recommended sites:

- Fiverr (fiverr.com) has 250-plus freelance types.

- Flexprofessionals (flexprofessionalsllc.com) is a staffing firm that matches professionals with part-time and flexible jobs.

- Freelancer.com connects employers and freelancers worldwide. Areas range from software development to writing, data entry, and design and from engineering, the sciences, sales and marketing, and accounting to legal services.

- GLG (glginsights.com) is a global network of fee-based executive-level experts. If you're accepted as a member, you're connected to paying clients for problem-solving and more. The network currently has more than a million top professionals and subject matter experts on board. Network members consult with clients over the phone or in person, through small group meetings, longer-term projects, or board opportunities.

- Jobspresso.co is a Canada-based site frequented by US workers that concentrates on remote opportunities.

- LinkedIn Jobs (linkedin.com/jobs) is a fast-growing and robust platform with more than 30 million businesses posting openings on the professional networking site with remote positions as one of the filters you can set.

- The National Telecommuting Institute (ntiathome.org) is a nonprofit that works with the Social Security Administration to match telecommuting jobs with people who have disabilities.

- PatinaNation.com focuses on independent executives and managers who have 25 or more years of experience and are looking for part-time projects or gigs.

- Ratracerebellion.com has been at the forefront of the work-from-home revolution since 1999.

- Remote.co is a site created by the founder of FlexJobs.com.

- Sidehusl.com reviews and rates online platforms geared to job opportunities. Click on what work you want to do to see the options.

- SkipTheDrive.com is targeted at full- and part-time telecommuting jobs.

- The Acceleration Project (TAP) (theaccelerationproject.org) is a female-founded, female-led business advisory firm dedicated to supporting underserved small businesses, with a focus on those owned by women and people of color. TAP hires consultants to team up with business owners to solve problems in areas including strategic planning, marketing, financial management and operations, and branding and positioning in the marketplace.

- Toptal (toptal.com) is a global network that promotes and places freelance software developers, designers, finance experts, product managers, and project managers.

- UpWork (upwork.com) has millions of job postings with 5,000 skills across more than 70 types of work.

- VirtualVocations.com offers access to the site's job listings of more than 40,000 remote jobs for free.

- WeWorkRemotely.com has programming, sales, and other jobs.

- Work At Home Vintage Experts (wahve.com) is a contract staffing firm that places older professionals in work-from-home positions in the insurance, accounting, and human resources fields.

- Working Nomads (Workingnomads.co/jobs) lists tech, management, marketing, and other jobs.

- Ziprecruiter.com lists millions of jobs, searchable by categories such as work from home, part-time remote, stay-at-home mom, and more.

When exploring these sites for potential jobs, keep in mind these two tips:

1. Check to see if the boards screen and vet the employers listed. This is critical, in my opinion, since there are still plenty of scammers out there who look to take advantage of unsuspecting workers seeking remote jobs and projects.

2. You also might go straight to a company you'd like to work for and see if there are remote openings listed on its website.

Applying for a Remote Job

Although remote work is almost, dare I say, conventional now, when you're being considered for a remote position, you need to go that extra step to reassure and convince a hiring manager that you're worth that leap of faith. You already have lots of the skills in your quiver that will make it work for you. These include organizational skills, an aptitude for laser focusing, discipline, communication skills (both verbal and written), a gift for time management, and an ability to work without a lot of supervision.

Moreover, landing a remote job often relies on your ability to show a potential employer you've been there and done that, and chances are since the onset of Covid-19 you have some real examples to share, if you didn't before.

It's also quite likely that what was once considered a bar you needed to jump is no longer an issue—demonstrating tech skills. You've probably already done some refreshers on computer applications and communication tools, such as web conferencing, video chats, and other programs.

You'll want to be sure you highlight these things on your résumé, cover letter, and online profiles—including any contract and freelance work you've done. Include a specific checklist of remote technology you're now proficient with, such as instant messaging programs like Slack and Google Chat; file sharing on Dropbox; document collaboration on Google Drive; videoconferencing via Zoom, Microsoft Teams, GoTo Meeting, and Skype; and other remote collaboration tools such as Asana.

REMOTE WORK ISN'T FOR EVERYONE

To be fair, not everyone is hardwired to work from home. It's not a matter of navigating the technology, which, as we know, is one of those myths about older workers. It's the human connection and the network and camaraderie that makes some people feel valued and engaged in their work.

Digital burnout is undisputable for those who have trouble shutting down and drawing boundaries with their bosses and coworkers. And it can be a dreaded nightmare for those who find the communication channels awkward. I know many workers who routinely misread expectations and fail to have those tough conversations to make sure they are on the same page with their manager or team. It's frustrating. Everyone loses.

HOW TO SUCCEED IN A REMOTE JOB

Self-discipline is the secret sauce to success. You need to be clear-eyed about this, however, because it is harder than it sounds. You must create limits around your work environment with friends, family, and neighbors, as well as your boss, colleagues, and team members, to avoid the burnout I just referred to.

And there are psychological stumbling blocks to remote work as well. One of the biggest is loneliness. The very best remote workers will reach out to coworkers and managers frequently. A key skill companies that hire remote workers are looking for is communication—particularly about work concerns or challenges. You need to be able to say, "I'm a little baffled about this" or "Can you clarify this for me?" The best remote workers speak up. If you're not eyeball to eyeball, it's hard for your manager to know if something is off-track.

Regular conversations—by phone, text, email, or video chats—may be your only way to share the development of your projects. Catching up with your supervisor through a weekly virtual or one-on-one phone call can give you both a chance to connect even if there isn't a specific work agenda to review. It's human nature and often subliminal for bosses to be wary when employees are out of sight, so protect yourself by sharing.

The underlying issue of trust from your boss is hard to pinpoint or measure, but believe me this is eternally essential to nurture. Meet your deadlines and beat expectations. Raise your hand for assignments that might be a little scary, but will add skills and experience.

Succeeding as a remote worker takes consistent cultivating, but for many people, like me, it's the perfect way to accomplish a balanced approach to creative work. And for those of you easing your way into retirement, or working part-time in retirement, the flexibility to work remotely is a huge reward and one that is worth using extra energy to get right.

But I do suggest flourishing as a remote worker requires you to make a few other moves in your daily routine.

Get out of your pjs. When you dress up, even just a bit, it can change your attitude. You put on your work identity and energy seems to flow faster. For me, it's typically a nice pair of stretchy black pants (not leggings or yoga pants), a top I'd be comfortable wearing into the office, and flats.

If your work will require a deeper digital skill dive, check out training available on online from your local library, LinkedIn Learning, Coursera, Udemy, and YouTube. Search "remote work" on LinkedIn Learning, for example, and you'll locate online classes for workers and managers. Microsoft provides on-demand training videos for its apps. Google provides workshops for its office apps suite, including Docs, Sheets, and Slides. GetSetUp.io offers live classes for adults on everything from Excel Basics to Zoom protocol.

Home Office Dos and Don'ts

Some basic setup in your home office will make a difference in your comfort during the workday and your productivity. The right computer monitor or laptop, chair, lighting, and laptop stand can help. The *New York Times* Wirecutter site (nytimes.com/wirecutter /office/home-office) has some useful ratings for home office furniture and supplies.

Keep an eye out for home office mess. It can be a drag on your output. Even an electronic mailbox with way too many saved messages or flags to remind you to get back to a person can suck your get-up-and-go. Think organizing consultant Marie Kondo and tidy it up.

I like to arrange my desktop before I shut down for the night. Every day or so I wipe my browser of cookies that have been stored there by websites I've tapped into. Simple routines.

I also have pictures of my animals and family members as well as a beautiful painting of an old-fashioned log cabin my family owned when I was a kid. It's my dream house, with streams running alongside it. When I need to, I stare at it. Then close my eyes. It calms me down; I feel peaceful and my attitude shifts.

I suggest putting your central image in a place where you physically must turn away from your computer to look at it. The very act of directing your attention away from your work opens the door in your day for a breather. It's revitalizing.

Setting Up Your Computer

Since you will be face to "computer face," I want to remind you of a few computer setup basics. You'll need a fast internet service, a webcam (usually built into your computer), and a microphone (again the one on my MacBook Air works just fine). You might invest in an external USB microphone like a high-quality Blue's Snowball. A USB lavalier microphone is another option. It clips to your clothing about three inches below your chin on your right side (ideally on a shirt or jacket collar).

Check out the background your virtual callers will see. If possible, I do this immediately after I sign into a meeting and before it starts. Zoom allows you to do a check ahead of time. That lets me see how I have the screen positioned, tilt it down for less head room, or maybe slide my chair for optimal positioning and to avoid the window light. You want your background to enhance you, or at the very least not draw attention away from what you have to say.

I have windows in my office, so lighting can be thorny. The bottom line is that you want soft light in front of your face. If your room has a window, you might sit in front of it. I keep two desk lights on, and I also use a ring light or Lume cube set up behind the center of my computer screen.

Always check that you're in the middle of the screen and the top of your head is close to the top of the computer screen. You should look slightly upward at the camera lens, which if it is embedded in your screen, is also at the top center. This angle gives you a defined chin and subtly indicates self-confidence. To get the right level, I pile up a few books under my laptop, but you'll find your own method. (I'm aware that I reviewed these setups in the last chapter on your virtual interviews. I'm not losing it folks, these are just remote working rules of the road.)

I generally put sticky notes around the edges of my computer screen and on the lampshades of my desk lights to remind me of talking points for each call or meeting I'm in. It makes it easy to remember these without looking down and away from the contact with my eyes on the camera. Again, not everyone is such a stickler for looking into the camera directly, but I prefer to do that.

It is especially tempting to glance at yourself on the screen or the thumbnails of other participants—but keep it to a minimum. Stick a note to yourself next to the camera lens as a reminder to keep your focus.

And even in the most serious meetings, slip in those smiles. Smiling boosts the conversation. And makes you feel more engaged and motivated.

"Shoulders back" is another note to consider posting as a reminder. Posture conveys a message about who you are and how invested you are in the conversation.

Pay attention to any physical tics you might have that are distracting to the person or people on the other side of your virtual conversation. I'm thinking about twisting your hair, chewing gum, or scratching. I know this sounds so basic, but we all forget there is a person with eyes glued on us sometimes when they aren't physically with us.

If something goes askew—say, your internet connection gets shaky or the dog next door won't stop barking—better to acknowledge it, so it's not so annoying.

Stay Healthy

You are what you eat. What does nutrition have to do with succeeding in the new world of work? A heck of a lot. When you work from home, it's normal to find yourself grazing on a handful of candy or chips. Don't get me started on the kettle corn. I do my best to keep apples and clementines in the fridge and a full bottle of water close at hand.

Make it a habit not to miss meals. Without a lunch buddy, it's easy to plow on through the day without that pause to regroup and refill.

My point here is that self-care is the undercurrent that will allow you to thrive as a remote worker. Take a walk outside, even if you don't have a dog. Go for a bike ride. Practice yoga or mindful meditation. Read a book or magazine or really anything that has nothing to do with your job.

Step away from your office space. Pick up the phone and call someone for a quick catch-up. Sip a cup of herbal tea or hot chocolate with some marshmallows on your deck if you have one.

Take a gym break to work out or tap into a wellness app like Headspace (headspace.com), Calm, or Happify (happify.com). Turn on some music and dance around the kitchen. (I confess I like to blast the Rolling Stones or Bruce Springsteen and just dance like no one's watching . . . and they aren't! Elly with her tail wagging madly does join me sometimes.) Any of these activities—or ones that I didn't mention—that call to you can make a huge difference in your mental acuity and your ability to navigate the new world of work.

Old-Fashioned Phone Calls Are Still OK

Final note: I have enjoyed the independence of remote work for years, but I personally do everything I can to avoid a video Zoom or Google Meetup when it's appropriate, especially if it's just with one person. An old-fashioned phone call where I can walk around while I talk really makes me happy, and I feel smarter, empowered, and more energized. Goofy maybe, but true. And that way, I don't need to bother with hair, makeup, lighting, microphone setup, and all those other time zappers that go into preparing for that tête-à-tête. Just sayin'. You might find some of your own tricks and workarounds that help take control of the unrelenting virtual meeting klieg light.

8

Career Transition

I spend a lot of time talking to audiences and writing about what we do with our working lives, ways to love our jobs, and how we can make a difference in our lives and have a positive impact on the world around us.

One factor that can contribute to embracing your work—and it's becoming increasingly prevalent in today's workplace—is making a career transition to do something new, something you're passionate about, or something you've always wanted to try.

Changing careers is rapidly becoming mainstream. And it's not just the outliers taking risks. Today, workers of all ages are stepping off the traditional linear path. Instead, it's a bit more like a patchwork quilt. Jobs are more fluid. Career paths in the new workplace are and will continue to be more creative and improvisational.

You might do something new for a decade or more, or only a couple of years, and then shift to something completely different once again. The beauty of it is there *is* a road map to guide your shift without making a rash, emotional decision. I will show you how to make this a prudent, planned course of steps that will set you up for both personal and professional success. No two paths are the same, of course.

I've interviewed or worked directly with hundreds of workers who have shifted gears, some dramatically, some more subtly, and I know what it takes to make it work. If there's something inside of you calling you to make a change, I believe you should follow your heart and your gut. It might be a passion you've felt for some time. Or, it may have been stirred out of necessity because your previous job "disappeared." Technology and the pandemic have brought extraordinary changes in our jobs, and the reality is that some jobs simply haven't survived, or are on their way out as the natural evolution of work.

REDEPLOY YOUR SKILL SET

Changing careers is a big deal, but it's absolutely manageable. Don't think of this as *reinventing* your career or making a massive change. What you're doing is *redeploying* your skill set. You're reimagining how to put the puzzle together in a new design. With all those tools in your wheelhouse, you can shift to a new direction. Sure, you will add new ones, meet new people, and have new challenges, but the core *you* is in place to anchor your pivot.

Take time to reflect on your motivation: Why are you making a switch? Why you, why now, and why this particular field, this kind of job? These profound questions get to the heart of what's motivating you.

If you're seeking a career transition because you're miserable at work, your boss is a jerk, you're not getting promoted, you're burned out, or, frankly, because you're bored, hold hard. Pay attention. Do you think this is the panacea for all that? Possibly. To me, that's generally not a recipe for success. Hit the pause button and think hard about the impetus for your desire.

The process can be challenging on several levels. First, change of any kind is stressful. It usually takes time. And you probably will suffer financially because you likely will have to take a pay cut as you begin your new career.

Are you making a career change for the *right* reasons? You should never make the shift because you're running away from something, but rather to move *toward* something positive, something that you wish to do, that means something to you. You want to embark on a career shift by stepping toward a goal you're excited about attaining. When you step into a change for a motive that is true to who you are and to enhance your well-being, it will give you the get-up-and-go and grit you need to make the turn.

CAREER TRANSITION ROAD MAP
WORKSHOP NOTES

Soul searching:

My strengths and skills are: _____

My passions are: _____

I am curious about: _____

I want to leave behind: _____

Activities I loved as a child:

• _____

• _____

• _____

What are my career change motivations?

Full-time income	Part-time income	Work with meaning	Flexible lifestyle
Take hobby to next level	Be my own boss		Be part of a team
Be creative	Develop new skills	Work on issues that matters to me	

Career ideas on my mind:

• _____

• _____

• _____

• _____

Contacts in field(s) of interest:

• _____

• _____

• _____

• _____

Career transition is a process. No rash moves. Don't get hung up on the daunting thought that you're *reinventing* your career. You're *redeploying* your skills.

Kerry Hannon | Career Transition Strategist
kerryhannon.com | linkedin.com/in/kerryhannon | @KerryHannon

CAREER TRANSITION ROAD MAP

Once you're straight on what's driving your desire to make a transition, examine your hard skills, maybe data analytics or marketing, and then your softer skills. Are you a great communicator? Do you have terrific writing skills, are you a superstar on your feet making oral presentations? Maybe it's your leadership skills that set you apart.

Own those skills and talents that are intrinsic to you and who you are. They are the underpinnings of your past success and will serve you well as you move forward in a new career. Embrace them.

All these abilities are moveable in new directions. Ultimately, you will want to have a go-to list of examples to show potential employers how these skills helped you solve a problem or helped your firm succeed and to suggest how these same skills can help the company you're interviewing with solve their unique challenges.

Once you suss these out, pull your toolkit apart and make sure you understand exactly what you're very good at and what your precise skill sets are. That way, you'll know exactly how to sell yourself to a new employer in a field where you may not have direct experience. A smart hiring manager knows that knowledge of the field matters, but it's skills, attitude, willingness, and curiosity to learn that are the soul of what makes a great employee and team member.

SEEK OUT A FELLOWSHIP

If you're looking for a job with a social purpose, consider applying for an Encore fellowship at Encore.org/fellowships (more information on Encore later in this chapter). These are up to one year paid fellowships at nonprofits. The selection process is a competitive one.

Why to Hire a Career Coach

Hiring a career coach is something you may want to consider, especially if you've lost a job during Covid-19 or were offered a voluntary early retirement package. A career coach can be a great sounding board and help you figure out what kind of work you can do next, how to become a top applicant, and how to get hired. Moreover, the advice is custom fit to you and your situation.

More big employers, in fact, are offering career counseling to help their employees find a new job after taking a voluntary buyout package or a layoff. But I recommend working with a coach at least for a period, even if you have to pay out of pocket. We already reviewed how to find one and what you might expect to be charged in Chapter 5.

Billy Spitzer, now executive director of the Hitchcock Center for the Environment in Amherst, Massachusetts, said career coaching helped him make a change after nearly 24 years with the New England Aquarium in Boston. In that job, he was responsible for public engagement, education programs, community partnerships, and other duties.

In 2020, Spitzer, then 58, chose to take what he calls "early retirement" during the initial months of the pandemic. "I was ready to think about what I wanted to do next," Spitzer said. "I needed a thought partner, and a colleague of my wife's recommended a coach she knew as someone to talk to."

Originally, Spitzer needed direction in thinking about his next stage. But he then looked for help "thinking about how do I want to present myself when I was looking for opportunities," he said. Spitzer, of course, hadn't looked for a job in more than two decades.

His Boston-based coach, Dorian Mintzer, encouraged him to ruminate "existential questions like: What makes a meaningful life?"

Spitzer told me when I interviewed him for Next Avenue. "It really helped me be open to different options and think less about 'there's job and there's retirement' and more like, 'well, there might be a different kind of job' and maybe the balance of work and personal life changes."

Mintzer also urged him to pinpoint his strengths. "It was a positive-psychology approach," Spitzer said. "We focused on the fact that I'm a really curious person and I love to learn and how I could make sure that came through when I was connecting with people."

For Mintzer, a good coach begins with the process of exploration and discovery. "It's giving somebody the opportunity to reflect on who they are and where they've been," she said. "What's their motivator, what interests them, and where are they now in this life stage?"

Mintzer frequently uses free Authentic Happiness questionnaires, which can be found on the University of Pennsylvania website developed by the Positive Psychology Center. Gallup's Clifton-Strengths is another assessment tool she recommends.

For some people, resources like those "actually can help them decide maybe they want to stay doing what they're doing," added Mintzer. "But they want to figure out if they can use their strengths in a different way. And asking is part of 'What's not been working for me that I haven't really been able to use in my strengths?'"

Mintzer has her clients make a list of all their skills from the different work situations they've been in, even a childhood job like delivering newspapers. "You can really get a sense of what are the skills that you have and what are the skills that you feel good about," said Mintzer. "This practice gets people thoughtful about using their skills in a novel way. You can then ask yourself: What are the ones that are transferable? What do I need to develop? What skills does the market need?"

Spitzer's work with Mintzer gave him a focused sense of what he prized at this stage in his career and what was useful when he was negotiating for his new position with flexible hours so he could have more life-work balance.

"Having a thought partner, or coach, who asks open-ended questions to make you think and then hear yourself say the answer out loud helps," said Cecelia Gerard, an executive career coach based in Drexel Hill, Pennsylvania. "It puts things in perspective. And then through that process is a refinement until you put together a plan that helps them move forward."

Gerard generally begins working with a client by asking the question: What energizes you? "Based on what energizes someone, then we focus on that," Gerard said.

She follows up with questions such as: Which types of industries would you like to work with? Which kinds of roles do you want to be in? Who might be some of the people you'd like to connect with? What is your personal philosophy around the work that you do? And how do you want to leverage your professional experience to go in that direction?

Coach Gerard also helps clients create their career narrative for networking and interviews. "I encourage them to create accomplishment stories around each of their achievements," she explained. "And they're ready when someone asks them a question. Immediately, their accomplishments pop into their head for whatever the question is."

Finally, and this should not be dismissed lightly, a career coach can guide you as you step into your future work as a beginner again. Feelings will inevitably bubble up when lose your old work identity and begin to prepare a new one. It's not unusual to feel a form of depression even if you can't put it in words what it is. This is a human reaction to change at this very personal level. Yes, this is your profession, but we all know it is so much more than that.

TALK TO PEOPLE IN
THE INDUSTRY

Another essential step in moving into a new act is tracking down people you know who work in the industry you're interested in transitioning into. This is the boots on the ground research stage where you get the true insider view.

Put on your thinking cap: Whom do you know in this industry that you want to move into or who can introduce you to some insiders? Join a LinkedIn or Facebook group connected with that industry. Do a search on LinkedIn to see if you know anyone working for a certain company that appeals to you, or in a certain type of job that lights you up. Join alumni groups to expand your network of contacts. Follow experts in the new field on Twitter.

Set up informational interviews to learn from those you make contact with either through a formal introduction from a mutual contact or by bravely reaching out and hopefully getting their attention perhaps by finding something you might have in common culled from their LinkedIn profile. This might be a hobby or a passion, such as a love of horses, or maybe you are both alumni of the same college, university, or high school, or you're from the same town. (See Chapter 6 for more ideas.)

I'm from Pittsburgh. And I can't tell you how many people share a love of that city and helping a fellow 'burgher out. Same goes for my alumni outreaches. If anyone from Duke University, Shady Side Academy, or The Ellis School for girls sends me a note asking for career advice, I make the time to chat. Period.

If it's a virtual meeting or a phone call, keep these discussions short and sweet—no more than 20 minutes. In-personal conversations will understandably run a bit longer. Honestly, most people love to talk about their work and give guidance, and they usually are flattered to be asked to help someone, but it is important to be sensitive to how much time they have to talk.

This is an essential stage of your due diligence. It's the homework stage. Make it fun. Enjoy meeting new people and soaking up their knowledge and experience.

It's an easy skate. You're not selling yourself. You're not doing the old soft shoe to get hired. It's a conversation and it's not about you at all. It's about absorbing knowledge about the kind of work you're interested in and where the opportunities are likely to be.

You're the listener. I imagine my Labrador retriever, Elly, looking intently at me as she waits for a treat or a command. (More than likely it's the treat that triggers that adoration.) You're listening to hear what this individual loves about their job, how they got started, where they see the prospects in their field, and how your skill set could work in your favor to move in this direction.

Be curious! Ask questions and take notes. Always wrap up your visit by asking who else they think you should talk to in order to learn more. Follow up with a thank-you note that says how much you appreciated the time and mention one or two things they said that resonated with you.

In addition to these informational interviews, research job boards and the career sections of employers in the field you want to transfer to. Scrutinize what new skills and education are prerequisites for those positions. Are there some you should consider adding to your repertoire?

The job postings will clearly say what qualifications are essential. You can also review LinkedIn profiles of people who are already working in that field in a job that interests you and make a note of their backgrounds, education, and skills. You don't necessarily need to get a master's degree or any kind of advanced degree. You can add a certification. A lot of this education is virtual now via training courses and workshops.

While you'll get a lot from informational interviews and other sources, it's important also to sign up for Google alerts on a company or nonprofit where you'd love to work so you can stay abreast of any news about their products or industry and more.

TRAINING CAN HELP CAREER CHANGERS

For job seekers, if you're looking to switch careers, training matters a lot. In the research report, "Meeting the World's Midcareer Moment," published by Generation, a global employment nonprofit, 74 percent of people in midcareer who had successfully switched to a new career reported that the skills they learned in training were instrumental in landing new jobs. And three in four employers report training and certifications as providing the equivalent of relevant experience in a job when hiring.[1]

Look for a training or certification program that has a network of employers who have signed up to offer job interviews to those who are emerging from it. Reach out to graduates of these programs to get their insights.

TIPS FOR CAREER TRANSITIONS

And as mentioned previously, career transition often goes hand in hand with some trade-offs. No surprise that the report by Generation also found that some career switchers compromised in terms of their role and seniority. Many would have liked a higher role. They accepted less compensation, which was often linked to a lower-level role as well. Some compromised in terms of the sector. For example, they were looking to get into tech and couldn't, and so took a job in retail or whatever it might be. But the point is that they fired through it, even though in the first few months they were asking themselves deep questions about, "Should I be here?"

One of the best ways to ease the anxiety of making a career change is to dip your toe in part-time work or try a side gig if you have the luxury of doing so. The more time you give yourself to test it out, the better your chances are of making the shift without taking a hit to your income.

For example, as you move to the next phase of your career transition, look for a way to volunteer or moonlight. If possible, you want to do the job first at least in some fashion to get a sense if it's all it's cracked up to be. Something that sounds dreamy and wonderful may not be when you're actually doing it. Job shadowing or an internship is another way to get this inside view.

One of my favorite career visionaries is Dorie Clark, author and educator at Duke University's Fuqua School of Business. When I asked her for her best advice for career changers, she told me: "It can take a while for a new career direction to get off the ground. In the period before it's clear that you've succeeded, it can often feel like a dark tunnel—are you making progress at all? How much longer? It can be a frustrating and discomfiting time, and that's when so many people quit prematurely."

Instead, Clark suggested "looking for the raindrops" by "making a conscious effort to identify small signs of progress, so you can both celebrate them and validate that you're on the right track. They might seem insignificant—'Big deal, five people signed up for my newsletter today.' But when you're just getting started, having five more people who are interested today, as compared to zero last week, actually is a big deal—and a small piece of evidence that your message is starting to resonate."

Finally, consider my fitness plan, particularly the money piece. Regardless of your financial situation, it's critical to have a grip on just how much money you need to earn now. When you're financially fit, you can take a chance at starting over in a new career. When you're dependent on earning a certain paycheck to pay the bills, you are locked in and that can limit your ability to move in a new direction.

Self-care is imperative. Physical and spiritual fitness will make the career transition smoother. Staying positive and balanced will go a long way in helping you stay the course and make connections.

Mindfulness training, which is now easy to tap into via your laptop or smartphone with apps like Calm and Headspace, can help you become more open-minded and develop a more agile approach to your work and job search.

"The ability to adapt to a rapidly changing world is fundamental to career and financial survival," said Jeff Tidwell, cofounder of Next for Me, an online resource that connects those 50+ through "new work, a new purpose, or a new social contribution." "Those left standing in the tsunami of workplace change we are undergoing must have an ability to successfully 'surf' career transitions," he told me.

Career shifts come in all shapes and sizes. A career shift at midlife can be big and bold. I know someone who went from being a retired Navy pilot in his mid-50s to a company manager of a circus troupe.

There's the botanist who became a chocolatier or the CNN producer who launched a winery.

FROM FELLOWSHIP TO FULL-TIME JOB

But some shifts are more subtle. At 54, Edgar Maxion, for example, had spent more than 20 years as chief facilities officer at Stanford University managing a burgeoning roster of construction projects.

"I was doing eight projects at once," Maxion said. "I wasn't seeing straight. I couldn't even sleep at night." But he wasn't ready to stop working. "In my heart of hearts, I wanted to be in a position where I felt like I was helping someone, as opposed to just getting a paycheck," he said. "I'm thinking: How do I help if all I only know about is building systems?"

While exploring job and volunteering posts on the nonprofit job site Idealist, he noticed Encore.org—a nonprofit that taps the skills and experience of people in midlife and beyond—and its Encore Fellowships program. That program matches skilled professionals looking to transition their skills to assist social sector organizations. They generally do it full-time for 6 months or part-time for 12 months, earning a stipend of $25,000 for 1,000 hours.

"Encore Fellowships were created as a way to reengage adults who had retired or been displaced from their previous jobs, providing them with a way to use their experience and earn a modest income while giving back," said Jim Emerman, Encore's vice president and national director of Encore Fellowships.

"The job loss and social isolation during the pandemic increased the number of older people looking for both work and purpose," Emerman added. "Simultaneously, nonprofits have never been hungrier for affordable strategic guidance. It's a win-win situation that will, hopefully, allow many seasoned professionals to pivot into the social sector and continue using their experience to drive social and environmental progress long beyond Covid times."

After Maxion filled out his application and met with an Encore counselor, he was matched with Sunnyvale Community Services (SCS), a Silicon Valley emergency assistance agency working to prevent hunger and homelessness. SCS wanted an Encore Fellow to manage the overhaul of a multimillion-dollar warehouse property the group had purchased. It was a smooth fit.

A month into Maxion's fellowship, the pandemic hit, and his assignment turned into a full-time facilities managing job. "While I was still trying to project manage this construction project, that actually fell off the wayside," Maxion explained. "The construction industry shut down for a bit, and rightfully so. Clients needed more help and SCS employees needed a safe space to work."

Maxion retrofitted SCS' 12,000-square-foot space for social distancing. He and his team modified the HVAC to expand outside air, increased janitorial service, bought personal protective equipment for the nonprofit's essential workers, and more.

Maxion's fellowship became a full-time job running the new 36,000-square-foot building renovation. The biggest reward: "It's a joy to help establish formats for the organization that will help them in the long run."

DO ONE THING EVERY DAY

One route to finding work in a new field is to look to small businesses, small trade associations, small nonprofits, even startups. Experience and sharp skills that are transferable trump industry know-how when these types of employers have a demand to get the job done and solve problems with scarce resources.

They value your experience, knowledge, and skills in a way larger firms enamored with hiring younger workers they have the time to get up to speed and can pay less don't. These kinds of small operators want someone who can do the job now.

Often, what it all comes down to is your inclination to be inquisitive and open to new fields and to make the effort to assess the skill set that the employers have in mind. Then compare that to what you have and be creative in ways you can apply your skills in a new avenue.

It's getting out of your lane and unsettling at times. It's easy to doubt yourself and your ability to make it happen. But in today's workplace, it can be what's best for you in the long run.

There is never an ideal time to get started on a career change, so my best advice is to start in baby steps through the map I've just outlined for you. Just get underway. Do one thing every day to move forward and stick to it. The runway will unfold as you build momentum toward what's next.

9

Be Your Own Boss

When I started my own business in my 40s, I admit it was scary, and it took a few years to get my income back to where it had been previously. But guess what? The psychic and emotional rewards of being my own boss and controlling my schedule are impossible even today to put a dollar figure on. They are priceless.

Being in charge of whom I work for and when and where is a dream. It's empowering and liberating. I can still remember my last in-house job and that horrible feeling of being trapped, resentful of not being allowed to write stories that were my ideas because they weren't in my "beat." I had to drag myself to the office to even get there by 10 a.m.

It was a cacophony in the enormous newsroom with no buffering walls and reporters jammed together. I would watch the clock to see how soon I could escape. The anxiety was palpable. And then one day I quit and took off to New Mexico to write a book about Navajo weavers.

Stepping into your own business isn't for everyone. I get that. But for workers over 50 in today's workplace it's increasingly common and will continue to be so. The digital explosion into every aspect of our working lives has enabled that. You can work virtually and run your show from home or wherever you may be.

Your work might be as a freelancer, contractor, or consultant. It might involve a full-blown bricks-and-mortar storefront or manufacturing a product. Whatever its scope, it's all yours. You own it. And the days of stressing over promotions and low pay, or grappling with job application rejections are behind you.

Before you get too far down the dreamy path of following a passion, there's some work ahead. First, ask those central questions about the business you want to start: Why me? Why now? Why this product or service?

Your answers matter. This is your ultimate inner why. It's important to be able to easily determine what distinguishes whatever it is you want to start.

MIDLIFE ENTREPRENEURS

The entrepreneurial movement started by Gen Xers and baby boomers has been gaining steam for several years now, but today it is driven by the massive economic shifts caused by the pandemic. If you experienced burnout and high level of stress, the prospect of being your own boss is positively liberating. Work-life balance has become a front and center priority. When you're your own boss, you can have that.

The significance of entrepreneurship, or self-employment as a form of work, rises significantly with age, according to a report by Cal J. Halvorsen and Jacquelyn B. James of the Center on Aging & Work at Boston College.[1]

"While about one in six workers in their 50s are self-employed, nearly one in three are self-employed in their late 60s and more than one in two workers over the age of 80 are self-employed," Halvorsen and James wrote.

For many workers over 50, "starting a new business by repackaging the skills and experience honed for decades into a new career is exciting," said Nancy Ancowitz, a New York City–based career coach.

"It hits you, especially during the coronavirus crisis, that time no longer feels unlimited," Ancowitz said. "You're aware of your own clock ticking. Since you don't have a seemingly endless vista of work ahead of you, you may be motivated to finally retool and learn a new trade, or just try something different."

A buyout sum from an employer can be the seed money to fuel a venture you've been contemplating.

"For many of my clients, it's that kick start rather than having to hunt for a job, with all of the loneliness and fear of rejection that comes with it, especially when they haven't looked for a job in ages," Ancowitz said.

The diversity of businesses started by people in midlife is strikingly varied—from selling nuts, bicycles, or jewelry to building websites or operating a food truck. I've been tracking boomer and Gen X entrepreneurs for more than a decade now, and I always smile when they tell me they just wish they had done it sooner.

"You can either see a world full of possibilities or a world full of obstacles," Simon Sinek, author of *The Infinite Game*, has said. "Entrepreneurs are the ones who focus on the thing they want to create or build, rather than focusing on all things standing in their way."

Studies show that entrepreneurs at midlife tend to have the highest success rates of any age group. A 50-year-old founder is 1.8 times more likely to achieve upper-tail growth than a 30-year-old founder, according to MIT economist Pierre Azoulay.[2]

Older entrepreneurs like you have a quiver of arrows to work with including management, marketing, and finance experience, and deep industry knowledge. Also—and this is significant—you may have more financial resources to tap and larger social and professional networks to reach out to for help. And if you're starting a business in a field where you have work experience, all the better.

Intergenerational Businesses

You might even launch your business alongside someone younger, like your daughter, as Edith Cooper did.

"Many seniors are building legacy businesses alongside a younger member of their family," Elizabeth Isele, founder of the Global Institute for Experienced Entrepreneurship, told me. "It's a winning formula for both generations."

Isele added: "When you're over 50, you often want to create a business that has social impact on your community, if not the world. And frequently the younger workers carry the same sense of idealism on their sleeves."

Cooper, who spent 20 years at Goldman Sachs, partnered with her daughter, Jordan Taylor, who was nearing 30, to cofound Medley, a career development platform based in New York City. They launched it during the pandemic.

To me, these intergenerational couplings exemplify a great strategy for future success. And you can expect to see more of these in the years ahead.

"Businesses that are staffed by multiple generations benefit from the different experiences and points of view that can make your business more responsive and more adaptable," John Tarnoff, executive, career transition coach, and author of *Boomer Reinvention: How to Create Your Dream Career Over 50* told me.

The 50+ entrepreneur often brings valuable years of experience, and the younger one counterpunches with the latest in technology skills and social media acumen.

A key benefit to founding a business with a family member who is decades younger is "the trust, commitment, and honesty that family brings," Kimberly A. Eddleston told me in an interview. She is professor of entrepreneurship and innovation at Northeastern University in Boston and professor of entrepreneurship and a senior editor on the EIX Editorial Board of the Schulze School of Entrepreneurship at the University of St. Thomas in Minneapolis. "Family members are often more honest and open with one another, which can help in identifying and solving problems." And when mistakes happen, Eddleston added, "They are quicker to forgive and move on."

It was Taylor's idea for a service to make executive-level coaching available to people at all ages and at all stages of their careers. Over two years, she and her mom honed the concept through discussions, exploration, and testing. Between its July 2020 launch and the fall of 2021, the women raised more than $5 million in capital. My guess is Cooper's extensive network helped with that.

Cooper said the benefit of running an intergenerational business is that "it leads to an incredible amount of creation, innovation, and learning from both perspectives." In hindsight, she told me, "When I was in a senior seat in my previous work, I always realized that 'Boy, did I have a lot to learn from the younger generations coming into the workplace every year.' The challenge is that you are coming at this from different perspectives. You have to be really intentional about not starting out a thought with 'Yeah, but if you knew what I knew.' That takes work."

The duo's advice for other intergenerational pairings: Focus on each of your separate gifts. "Big vision and an ability to draw connections—that's what Mom brings," Taylor said. Added Cooper: "I have worked in a variety of different environments with hugely different personalities. I see things that Jordan will eventually see, but it will take longer." And Taylor said her biggest asset is her attention to detail and capability to hold a lot of things organizationally in her head.

Learn from each other. "Go into the relationship intent on learning," Cooper advises. "To do that, you have to have an open mind and a fair amount of humility and the expectation that the other person has much knowledge that you don't have, regardless of the generational difference."

Be modest. Said Cooper: "There may be things I know given that I have had years more experience. But I also have years less experience in things that are native to Jordan, such as the leveraging of technology."

KEYS TO SUCCESS

Isele, a guiding light in this playing field, and I have spent hours munching French toast and sipping steaming mugs of coffee at a tiny wood-paneled restaurant in Sperryville, Virginia. We talk about what it takes to be an entrepreneur at this stage in life, the challenges and rewards. She launched SeniorEntrepreneurshipWorks.com, the precursor to The Global Institute for Experienced Entrepreneurship, in 2012 at the age of 70. "Senior entrepreneurship is redefining the future of work and traditional retirement across all generations, cultures, and geographic boundaries," she said.

The successful midlife entrepreneurs I have interviewed and worked with over the years share a common spine of smart moves they made to ensure their success:

- Those who succeed usually have an adaptable time span for their company to grow. They go slow. It can easily take a few years to get traction, and they plan accordingly both financially and personally.

- They did their research on the industry, the gaps they could fill. They added the essential skills, certificates, or degrees that were necessary before launching.

- They often apprenticed or volunteered beforehand with a comparable kind of job or business to see if it really is something that was as suited to them as they imagined.

- They reached out to their networks of social and professional friends and colleagues to ask for support and advice and sometimes help raising capital.

- They downsized and planned their financial lives so they could have enough money to get by until they were able to draw an income and to pay for the initial startup costs. Sometimes they were lucky to have a spouse's or partner's steady income or some independent investments, retirement savings, or pensions.

Some startups have grand goals and will require long hours and a weighty capital investment to succeed. Others can be simpler, such as a freelance consulting business or a craft shop on Etsy, a side gig making delectable macarons that you sell online while you work full-time as a veterinary technician. (Yes, that's you, Melissa at Melissa's Makery in Sperryville, Virginia.)

TALK TO OTHER BUSINESS OWNERS IN YOUR FIELD

Not unlike the kind of informational interviews someone might have when they are job hunting, you will want to reach out to business owners running companies in the same lane as you hope to launch in. You can learn a great deal and may even forge relationships that lead to cross-marketing or other types of shared promotions.

Halvorsen, assistant professor at the Boston College School of Social Work, an affiliate of the Center on Aging & Work at Boston College, told me, "Those who have higher levels of assets, spouses who have steady jobs, or families with a modicum of wealth are in a better place to start a business. If their ventures fail, they have something to fall back on."

But the advantage is notable. Older entrepreneurs, Halvorsen said, "gain a whole lot of flexibility in their work, and that's a major motivating driver for a lot of people. That does become more important the older you are. And they gain autonomy."

USE FREE RESOURCES

Check out the free resources available to you. The US Small Business Administration (SBA) has regional Small Business Development Centers and Women's Business Development Centers that offer state, local, and private grant information for those interested in starting for-profit or nonprofit businesses. SBA's WBCs are a national network of 136 centers that also offer one-on-one counseling and mentoring to women entrepreneurs.

SCORE (Score.org), a nonprofit affiliated with the SBA, also provides mentoring and educational workshops nationwide. SCORE publishes a free e-guide called "Where's the Money? 10 Most Popular Financing Sources and How to Qualify."[3]

AARP's Small Business website (aarp.org/work/small-business) is free resource. AARP and the SBA host events that offer counseling, training, and mentoring to see if you're ready to start a business.

Explore the free entrepreneurship resources at EIX.org. Entrepreneur & Innovation Exchange (EIX) is a free peer-reviewed resource on entrepreneurship and innovation for entrepreneurs, innovators, and those who support them such as investors, advisors, and educators.

The AARP Foundation's Work for Yourself @50+ (workforyourself.aarpfoundation.org/) offers free webinars and workshops as well as a downloadable toolkit with worksheets to help you set goals and more.

You can enroll in an online entrepreneurship course; many are free from universities such as Babson, Harvard, MIT, and the University of Maryland, and can be located on platforms such as Coursera and edX. The University of Pennsylvania's Wharton School online has a Coursera roster of free courses on entrepreneurship. LinkedIn Learning has a decent selection, too.

For those retiring, or transitioning from military careers, Boots to Business (sbavets.force.com/s/b2b-course-information) is an entrepreneurial program from the SBA that's part of the US Department of Defense Transition Assistance Program. It features an overview of entrepreneurship fundamentals and is open to transitioning service members (including the National Guard and Reserve) and their spouses.[4]

Pick up copies of my books, *Never Too Old to Get Rich, What's Next?* or *Great Jobs for Everyone 50+* (I couldn't resist) as well as Encore.org's vice president Marci Alboher's *The Encore Career Handbook*; Chris Farrell's *Purpose and a Paycheck: Finding Meaning, Money, and Happiness in the Second Half of Life*; John Tarnoff's *Boomer Reinvention: How to Create Your Dream Career Over 50*; and Nancy Collamer's *Second-Act Careers: 50+ Ways to Profit from Your Passions During Semi-Retirement*. All these books are inspirational and packed with resources.

DRAFT A BUSINESS PLAN

Create a solid business plan. Consulting with your financial advisor will give you a sense of what your personal assets are and what your options may be. Be certain that you have a good grip on the industry and those key questions: Why me? Why Now? Why this product or service? In essence, where is the need to fill a gap or solve a problem now?

In general, your business plan should include:

- An executive summary that states what your company will do, who the customers will be, why you are qualified to run it, how you'll sell your goods and services, and your financial outlook.

- A full description of the business, its location, your team, and your staffing needs. You should also have a section on your competitors.

- A market appraisal that describes your likely customers, including age, gender, and location. The analysis also will explain your sales and marketing strategy.

- An estimate of startup costs—including raw materials, equipment, employee pay, marketing resources, insurance, rent, and fees for professional services (say, attorneys and accountants)—and what you predict your revenues will be.

Believe in yourself and take your time.

Funding Sources

When Jenny Yaeger, then 55, launched her Denver-based accounting and financial consulting firm for small and medium-sized businesses, ClariFI Business Solutions, in spring 2021, she used her personal savings. "Downsizing was what made it possible for me to go out on my own," said Yaeger, former chief compliances and finance officer at Wakefield Asset Management.

Yaeger, who is divorced, purchased a condo with the proceeds from the sale of her home and had enough cash left over to cover startup expenses, such as purchasing equipment, hiring a coach to help with her business strategy, and joining a coworking space.

"Theoretically, my business can be run from my spare bedroom," she said. "But I've really found that I needed to be out and about. And being in the coworking space is great support and networking. There's a lot of women there building businesses; some have become clients and have referred me to others."

To jump-start her business coaching new writers through the self-publishing process—Nowata Press & Consulting—Dana Ellington, then 54, of Kennesaw, Georgia, pulled $30,000 from a retirement account. She had launched her company as a side hustle while working full-time as an office manager.

"I was not ready to take that leap full-time until the pandemic brought so many things into perspective," said Ellington. "The driving force was: I'm in my fifties, and if I don't do it now, when am I going to do it?"

When you're ready to launch, here's a rundown of the funding avenues to consider:

Personal savings. This is the primary way midlife entrepreneurs fund their new businesses. The truth is, especially with virtual businesses, you don't need to spend a fortune to get moving. "The costs of forming businesses have collapsed in many sectors, so the tap in to personal savings can be minimal, at best. You can spend a lot less than $10,000 to get off the ground," said Jon Eckhardt, University of Wisconsin School of Business professor and editor in chief of the Entrepreneur and Innovation Exchange (EIX) of the Schulze School of Entrepreneurship at the University of St. Thomas in Minneapolis.

You'll want to be vigilant to not exhaust any emergency funds you have socked away and be sure you don't need the funds for living expenses such as a mortgage. I can't emphasize this point enough: It's common to not draw a salary for at least a few months while your business grows or if you opt to reinvest earnings into it.

Friends and relatives. They love you! They frequently lend capital at low or no interest. Be certain to put the terms in writing so that there's no confusion about interest and repayment. Warning: Money can cause chaos on relationships should things not go smoothly.

Customer financing and consulting income. If your business will sell products, you can sell some of them ahead of production, according to Eckhardt. Also, he said, "You can earn early revenue by selling your time through consulting; use this revenue to finance the business and learn about your customer needs."

Banks and credit unions. Scoring a bank loan is a hair-pulling experience for many borrowers. There are lots of hoops to jump through from a paperwork perspective. And be aware they typically prefer to base a loan on your income as the barometer of your creditworthiness versus an asset-based one that takes into consideration your various investments, savings, and real estate holdings. A solid business plan and a top-ranked credit score are essential. You might approach a bank you already have a relationship with, or one familiar with your industry or known for small-business lending.

A bank that offers SBA-guaranteed loans with fixed rates is often a good route; check the Local Resources section of the agency's website (sba.gov). A lender may want you to put up collateral, typically a real estate asset. You will need to show that you have also invested in your startup and will put a down payment on your loan. Business.usa.gov is the federal government's site for entrepreneurs seeking short-term microloans and small-business loans. You'll find information on all programs open in your state.

Economic development programs. These are available in cities, counties, and states. The SBA's economic development department resources (sba.gov/about-sba/sba-locations/headquarters-offices/office-small-business-development-centers) can help you decide if this might be an avenue for you.

Angel investors and venture capital firms. This is a pipe dream when you're getting launched, generally speaking. Depending on your future ambitions, these kinds of investors can be good to have on your radar. These investors invest in your business, but also want a part of it—equity or partial ownership. One caveat for women: This might not be the best route because women get a fraction of venture capital globally, and those who are Black, Hispanic, or Asian get considerably less.

Federal government. Another source of venture capital is the SBA's Small Business Investment Company Program (sba.gov /funding-programs/investment-capital), which can provide an avenue for loans starting at $250,000.

You might also explore available grants at Grants.gov, which lists information on more than 1,000 federal grant programs. This is free money and not a loan, but it can be time-consuming to apply for and deal with the various hoops involved to wheeling your way through the red tape process in many instances.

Crowdfunding. Virtual fundraising campaigns on sites like Kickstarter, Indiegogo, and GoFundMe allow you to raise money for a new business in small increments—$10,000 would be a big haul. Find other businesses like yours that have crowdfunding campaigns and check out what levels they set for their goals. But if you're trying to crowdfund money this way, you'll need smart marketing chops.

It's not an investment, so the money is all yours, and it's a great way to build a customer base and mailing list, as well as get the word out in an organic grassroots way, particularly if you can share a product as a thank you for the contribution. Each of the big crowdfunding sites handles the funding process differently with various fees and percentages taken from credit card payments.

There are also a few crowdfunding platforms explicitly for female entrepreneurs, such as iFundWomen.

Equity crowdfunding. Equity crowdfunding platforms are another avenue to raise capital. Republic (republic.com), for example, allows investors—not just well-heeled ones—to invest in private startups that have been meticulously vetted, with as little as $10 or as much as $100,000 per investment. Unlike the traditional crowdfunding platform, people who invest expect a return, but you generally have time to let your company grow. Although this is called crowdfunding because they put together a bunch of smallish investors to help you, it is an investment not a goodwill "shucks I want to support you" kind of contribution.

"Within crowdfunding, there's a big difference between rewards-based crowdfunding and equity crowdfunding," said Daniel Forbes, an associate professor at the Carlson School of Management University of Minnesota and a senior editor on the EIX Editorial Board of the Schulze School of Entrepreneurship at the University of St. Thomas in Minneapolis.

"Rewards-based crowdfunding involves soliciting donations from people in exchange for some goods or services that will be made available at a future date. This has been an effective approach for entrepreneurs in cultural industries, like moviemakers or musicians," Forbes continued. "Equity crowdfunding, on the other hand, involves selling equity in your firm, and this is a more strictly regulated process."

Home equity loans or line of credit. This may be an easy route because the funds are usually taken as a lump sum that you can pay off over time at a low interest rate. If you have equity in your home and a credit score well above 700, it may be worth investigating.

And now the two sources of money to use with care:

Credit cards. Most cards carry double-digit interest rates, which is a huge price to pay for launching a business. If you take this option, shop for plastic with the lowest rates and best terms.

Retirement savings. Retirement accounts should be used with extreme caution. Generally, you don't want to dip into your 401(k) or IRA. Not only will you owe income taxes by taking money out, but you'll also lose the tax-deferred compounding and, if you're younger than 59½, you'll owe IRS withdrawal penalties. Worst of all, you'll potentially jeopardize your future financial security.

If you have a solo 401(k) already set up, you can borrow up to 50 percent of your vested account balance or $50,000, whichever is less. But here are some drawbacks. Interest on the loan is not tax-deductible. The funds you borrow are no longer invested, which may limit your opportunity for potential investment earnings. The loan must be repaid within five years of the date you receive the loan proceeds.

"Closing out the account didn't really bother me," Ellington explained to me. "I know a lot of people say you've got to plan for retirement, you've got to have the money. And, in the back of my mind, I guess I always see myself as working until I die. I am doing what I enjoy, willing to work harder at it, and I'm in it for the long haul. I've made it this far, and I trust myself to make it."

GET GOING AND GET HELP

Get your business rolling, even if it's part-time. Lenders consider your time actively working in the business when reviewing applications, and a track record is an advantage.

In today's virtual workplace, for entrepreneurs, hiring a virtual assistant can be a godsend. Six months after Tamara Schumer, of Fairfax, Virginia, opened her home-based window-treatment business, she was swamped with clients.

"I was fortunate," said Schumer, owner of Budget Blinds of Arlington & Alexandria. "But it was very stressful trying to handle customer service, scheduling, follow-up, orders, sales—all of that on my own."

So, she hired a few virtual assistants to take on some of her responsibilities. "I needed somebody to answer my phone and my emails," Schumer said. "I have an answering service, but they were very impersonal. I wanted to teach someone enough about the business so they could help me screen the calls and qualify the opportunities."

Schumer tapped FlexProfessionals (flexprofessionalsllc.com), a recruiting and staffing firm for the Boston and Washington, DC, areas, to help her find the right fit for her business. She started with a virtual office manager. "She answers the phone, schedules, and protects me from myself," Schumer said. "If I answer the phone, I'm always saying yes to the customer and overscheduling myself. She handles customer service issues and reorders, so I can really focus on the revenue generation. It has been hugely helpful."

Next, Schumer brought on a remote part-time bookkeeper. Although Schumer was formerly an administrative vice president at M&T Bank, in charge of the accounting basics, she detests those types of tasks. "This is my second career, and I wanted to have fun with my work. I'm spending money to have these women support me, but it's enabling me to focus on the sales," Schumer said.

"Our phone rings daily with calls from small businesses, many of whom are solopreneurs, stressing as their businesses take off," said Gwenn Rosener, partner and cofounder of FlexProfessionals. "Some are running around with their hair on fire, trying to juggle everything from accounting to marketing to tax filing and not doing any of it well. Some are locked in paralysis; they have so much to do they can't figure what to focus on, how to take a step forward."

One thing entrepreneurs I interview frequently tell me is that, when they look back at what they would have done differently launching their businesses, they wish they'd delegated tasks sooner. But getting yourself to do this is hard. It's easy to get into the superman or superwoman attitude that only you know what needs to be done and in a certain way. Meantime, bumpy revenue (particularly in the early days) can make it difficult to validate the expense.

If you do want to delegate some work, you can post a position on your industry association site or reach out to staffing agencies such as Boldy or FlexProfessionals, Work at Home Vintage Experts (WAHVE), FlexJobs.com, Upwork, and We Work Remotely. You can also post a virtual job opening on social media platforms, like a Facebook industry group, or do a search on LinkedIn ProFinder for the right freelancer for you.

WHEN CLIENTS ARE SLOW TO PAY

One of the most nerve-wracking things about being self-employed is dealing with clients who drag their feet on paying you, or run out on payment entirely. I was only stiffed once, thankfully. And it was one of the biggest media companies in the country. Needless to say, I have never accepted an assignment from that client again.

Most self-employed freelancers have problems getting paid at some point, according to research by the Freelancers Union (free lancersunion.org), the nonprofit group that promotes the interests of independent workers through advocacy, education, and services.

The best way to stop this from happening is to do a background check on the potential client *before* you agree to the assignment or project. Do you know anyone who has worked for them? What has their experience been with timely payment?

If you feel comfortable, you might ask privately in a members-only online LinkedIn or Facebook freelance group (or an independent workers group associated with your field) what others have experienced with that client. For me, on Facebook, that might be Binders Full of WRITING JOBS, a private group "for women and gender non-conforming writers of all backgrounds to share freelance, remote, part-time, and full-time PAID opportunities for fellow writers/editors." It has more than 30,000 members.

If you're doing your own billing and are not part of an online talent platform such as Patina (patinasolutions.com), Toptal (toptal .com), Upwork (upwork.com), or WAHVE (wahve.com), who will do the paperwork for you and collect the money, along with their cut, you need to be diligent about your bookkeeping and stay on top of what's outstanding.

I generally give clients a 30-day grace period, but for speaking engagements, I require half up front when I sign the contract and half after the event. It is not out of the ordinary, though, to ask to be paid a portion up front or in several payments throughout the work progression. I do this for my book deals.

Get a contract. Skip the verbal handshake. Ask for an agreement in writing that you both sign that outlines the project, your pay, and when it is due.

You can create your own contract if the client doesn't provide one. The Freelancers Union has a link on its website to walk you through the process of setting up a customized freelance contract. If it is a substantial project, you might hire a lawyer to vet it for you. I only use a lawyer to scrutinize book contracts.

Be certain up front that you have the contact information of the person in accounting that will deal with your contract and payment.

Set up a regular billing system. What works for you will depend on the kind of work you do. I generally invoice when a project has been completed and accepted, but longer-term projects may require a different approach with periodic payments that have been agreed upon in the contract, as suggested above.

Be aggressive about following up if a payment is late. Start with an email and then move to a phone call. But be tenacious. And save all documentation of your attempts to get your payment in full.

Hiring a lawyer to collect for you is a last resort. It can be costly and a hassle. A law, known as The Freelance Isn't Free Law, in New York City, requires that for jobs paying $800 or more, freelancers must be paid either by a specified date or within 30 days of completion. The law mandates double damages and attorney fees be awarded if a case goes to court and the judge rules in the freelancer's favor.

Wouldn't it be great to see this law passed in other cities and states? If you only do one thing, report the deadbeat client to the Better Business Bureau.

HOW TO MARKET YOUR BUSINESS

Another common refrain I hear from entrepreneurs 50+ when asked about what they would have done differently before they launched is they wish they had more sales experience. Even if you plan to hire someone to help you with sales and marketing, it still comes down to you.

Here are some sales tactics to help you market your business solo. Look for Help Wanted postings by potential clients on online websites like Upwork.com, Freelancer.com, VirtualVocations.com, TaskRabbit.com, and LinkedIn (linkedin.com/services). And advertise your own offerings there as well for someone who might be cruising for a professional who offers what your business does.

Set up company or professional pages on LinkedIn, Facebook, and Instagram. If you have a consumer product, do some stalking and see where competitors are posting their wares for customers to ogle. If you make a product, you can spotlight it on these pages. Sharing pictures of completed projects or products for satisfied customers. You might post a video of a work project from start to finish.

One of my favorite Irish designers is Maureen Lynch (maureen lynch.ie/). I discovered her work on one of my many trips to Ireland years ago, but now find myself ordering her pieces online from her website. I admit what has spurred me to do so are her 40-second videos in which she hammers away on a silver bangle or pendant and posts on Facebook and Instagram. They remind me of Ireland and the small horseshoe-shaped Sandycove Beach in Dublin Bay, where she lives and works and regularly swims. She posts pics of that, too!

Join a trade association affiliated with your line of work. Word of mouth is perhaps the most persuasive sales tool. Review association job boards and let other members know you're available for jobs. You can even offer your services complimentary too and ask for references in return.

Self-employed workers often have websites where they list fees. You can also reach out to peers and see if they are willing to share ballpark figures of their typical price lists.

A website will help you pull in customers, and it's a place where you can be "found" easily. It's your own piece of virtual real estate to tell everything about you and your work and share all those lovefest notes from customers who are crazy about you and your business.

TAKE CARE OF DETAILS

Running your own business from home allows you to open and close the shop at will. You can walk your dog anytime you want. I do. It clears my mind and makes for a happy dog, too. But there are some general steps that you must do that aren't as prosaic.

Secure the applicable permits—tax registrations, business and occupational licenses, and state and local government permits. If you belong to a homeowners association, make sure there aren't any restrictions to running a business out of your house.

Update insurance policies. It's generally a smart idea to add an insurance rider to your homeowners or renters policy to cover any expense should someone get injured on your property who is there for business purposes. Each state has its own rules about insurance. The Insurance Information Institute (iii.org), an industry trade group and information clearinghouse, is a place to begin your inquiry.

Set up quarterly estimated federal taxes on business income each quarter. Depending on where you are situated, it may be necessary to pay state and local income and business taxes, too. The IRS Self-Employed Individual Tax Center is a great resource to learn more, and, of course, make sure you have a trusted accountant on board.

You should, for example, be able to take a tax deduction for 100 percent of expenditures directly related to your home office, such as the purchase of a work computer. The other kind of tax-deductible home office outlays are "indirect" ones that are prorated, based on the square footage of your home and office. These are things like your mortgage or rent, insurance, and utility bills. To get the deduction, you must file Form 8829, Expenses for Business Use of Your Home. For full details, go to IRS Publication 587.

LEAD A BALANCED LIFE

Stick to a regular work schedule if at all possible. I personally work early mornings but avoid evening hours. That's easier said than done, but it's important to create a balanced work environment.

Vaccinated folks should look for occasions to connect in person with clients or colleagues for coffee or a meal. Attend industry seminars, go to conferences, and pop into local Rotary Club lunch meetings where other small-business people convene. Virtual ones, too, can give you a boost and help with networking and spread the word about your business. At the very least, call someone or have a Zoom chat in lieu of texting or sending an email. It's energizing.

Running a home business can be lonely in the best of times. Creating a support group of other work-at-home entrepreneurs can be a solution. Russ Eanes, in his 60s, founded the editing and self-publishing business Walker Press and operates it from his home office in Harrisonburg, Virginia. He gets companionship and ideas by getting together with a small cadre of five other business owners. "My group meets virtually once per week," said Eanes. "We learn from each other's successes and failures. It helps that I don't feel it's just 'me, myself' out there."

One element to the positive group interaction is that they are not competitors: "We are involved in different types of work, so there is a cross-fertilization of ideas," Eanes said.

I find these groups a true salvation for solo entrepreneurs, specifically those facing trials when launching.

"I think it is a unique concept that can certainly serve as emotional support for struggling entrepreneurs," said Donna M. De Carolis, dean of the Charles D. Close School of Entrepreneurship at Drexel University and a member of the editorial board of EIX, the Entrepreneurial and Innovation Exchange, funded by the Schulze Family Foundation. "The idea of a diverse brain trust group to flesh out ideas and challenges is a good one."

I was taken by this concept, which has been a winning one for everyone from job seekers to women relaunching in the workplace in their 50s. So, I did some reporting for Next Avenue on what the secret sauce to making one of these jive for entrepreneurs working from home. This is some of the advice I gleaned.

Look for entrepreneurs at a similar stage of business growth as yours. "The key is to have some commonality among the members," said Marc Miller, founder of CareerPivot.com. "In my group in the Career Pivot Community, everyone is early in their journey and is building largely a solopreneur business. They can help one another stay out of their heads, and, more importantly, be cheerleaders for one another."

Outside input "keeps you grounded," Miller noted. "When you get discouraged, you may need someone outside of your sphere to pick you up."

And the participants could become allies. "I have a number of people in my group who have partnered up to either work on projects together, or used each other as a resource," Miller said.

Stay small. "The goal is to bring together around 5 to 10 entrepreneurs on a regular basis—once a week or once a month," said Fran Hauser, a New York City area-based startup investor and advisor as well as author of *The Myth of the Nice Girl: Achieving a Career You Love Without Becoming a Person You Hate*. "It's easier than ever now to run a virtual meeting for an hour over Google Meet or Zoom, which allows you to invite entrepreneurs who don't live in your town to join," she said.

Create a varied group. When cherry-picking members seek out diversity in terms of ethnicity, gender, age, and personality types. This will bring differing viewpoints and stimulate conversation. To find members, tap into your LinkedIn connections, Facebook friends, your alma mater alumni group, and even your local Chamber of Commerce.

But Miller added a caveat: "It is valuable to have slightly different skill sets and experiences, but you also need chemistry between the members. I was asked to be part of a group a few years back. I went for about a month and found there was not a commitment from others to show up. And more importantly, I did not like several of the members personally. They were either too judgmental or critical of others. That was not the kind of environment I wanted to be around."

Consistency is important. "I like to meet weekly because I need someone to hold me accountable," Miller said. "Anything over a week in between meetings—it becomes difficult to do that."

A steady check-in can be vital for your mental health as well as business counsel, particularly when your business is just getting off the ground. "In the initial stages of entrepreneurship, it's imperative because that's a period full of unknowns, self-doubt, and in many unfortunate cases, loneliness," Nathalie Molina Niño, author of *Leapfrog: The New Revolution for Women Entrepreneurs* and cofounder and managing director at Known Holdings, told me. "It's about connecting."

Setting up an agenda can be useful. This keeps the meetings focused. In Hauser's group, she said, "The members each share something they're working on or struggling with, and the other members respond with thoughts."

Two parting thoughts from a conversation I had with Alisa Cohn, executive coach and author of *From Start-Up to Grown-Up*. "Your company becomes a mirror of yourself, with all the good and all the bad. Self-examination before a launch helps you identify what leadership qualities you have, what qualities you need, and how you are going to make the most of your strengths, bridge the gaps in your skills, and strengthen some of your weaknesses," she said.

"Second, in general, entrepreneurs are often known as control freaks, and only they can do it. The more you can delegate, the more successful you will be, even if everything is not always done perfectly perfect."

Career Advice for Women Over 50

Women over 50 had a precarious ride through the pandemic months. Work from home created a kind of work-life balance implosion that often manifested itself in stress and burnout, particularly if caregiving was one of the duties. It could be caring for adult children, grandchildren, aging parents, and/or other relatives.

Many women of all ages were unable or unwilling to juggle it all and chose to just step out of the workforce. They had to for their mental and physical well-being. Boomer and Gen X women put their careers on pause. They downshifted. Gallup analysis found that 500,000 more women than men left the workforce during the pandemic.[1]

In my case, I didn't quit work, but I was hanging by my fingernails and hardly sleeping. My 91-year-old mother with dementia lived with me for much of 2020 and was my caregiving responsibility. There is absolutely no way I could have completed my work projects without a flexible schedule. When she was awake, she was always front and center. I was delighted and honored to be there for her.

Bringing women back to work will require employers to amend their flexibility practice for certain and to find ways to support women's wellness. This will be key with hybrid workplaces and full-remote positions as well. Returnships such as Irelaunch and reacHIRE (reachire.com/), a program that partners with large companies to help women gain skills, training, and mentorship when they return to work after staying home to care for a family member, can help women get back to work and can be critical to making this possible.

CHALLENGES WOMEN RETURNEES FACE

Workplace roadblocks for caregivers are a reality for all ages. This is not new to the postpandemic work environment. Over the years, I have heard regularly from women in their 50s and 60s that they left their jobs to raise kids and later find themselves alone and drifting after the kids are launched and their husbands departed, either due to a death or divorce.

Some have told me leaving the workforce was the biggest blunder they ever made. That kind of remorse is rough to live with, and it's an honest truth.

For those who lose a job at this age, it can be a rude awakening. It was the shock wave of rejection letters from hiring managers that motivated Guadalupe Hirt and Barbara Brooks, both 50+, to launch SecondActWomen (secondactwomen.com), a Denver-based company designed to help working women in their 50s and older (and some in their 40s) start companies, pivot careers, and stay employed. "The hiring managers didn't even give us a chance," Brooks told me when I spoke to her for a Next Avenue column. (Brooks and Hirt were named 2021 Next Avenue Influencers in Aging.)

Both women had long careers as marketing and public relations strategists. Hirt's focus had been entrepreneurial, founding or cofounding four firms. Brooks had worked primarily for corporations.

"Most of our friends were in their 40s and 50s," Brooks told me. "And I had this aha moment—it was women over 50 saying they wanted to do their own thing. They wanted to live their own life. They were feeling invisible, instead of invincible."

The women's organization serves entrepreneurs all over the world who are starting up, looking to grow their business, or starting a side hustle, as well as corporate women who have been laid off and are looking to find a position. They host virtual and in-person peer-to-peer workshops, conferences, retreats, and intensive boot camps. Topics include finances and business planning, personal branding, and business branding.

"We're getting women to be proud of the age and chapter they are at," Brooks said. "This is who we are. We are adventurous and we are experienced. We are at the top of the hill, not over the hill. We are asking: 'What is the next thing I want to do when I grow up?' It's so powerful."

While all the job-hunting strategies that I laid out earlier are essential tools for all workers over 50, women must do the proverbial dancing backward in heels. Women over 50, and heck, probably over 40, face a twofold curse of both gender bias and ageism. Women are still paid less than men in many positions. And I am confident in saying that we typically don't have equal opportunities for advancement.

Sure, that's not news to you. It has been part of the fabric of your working life since you accepted your first job. But as you begin to show visible signs of aging when you skip over 50, 60, and beyond, you're observed through another lens, which is ageism, as are men, but because of the emphasis on looks or "lookism," as executive coach Bonnie Marcus (bonniemarcusleadership.com) calls it, we experience it earlier than men do.

"I think gendered ageism is under the radar, and we need to build more awareness, similar to the way we built awareness around sexism with #MeToo," Marcus said.

Don't Internalize the Negatives

I realize this sounds shallow, but there is such an emphasis on youth and beauty that women have internalized their entire lives that we begin to let those negative sentiments and body-shaming images cloud our sense of self-worth as we age.

We reflexively step away from drawing attention to ourselves by avoiding asking for new duties or challenging projects. We tolerate men talking over us in meetings and taking credit for our work or our ideas. We're so used to it that in the workplace, we don't even recognize it's happening.

It's been a steady numbness to it. But as the years pass it's harder than ever to break through.

Over a third of female senior leaders say they're interrupted or spoken over more than others, compared to 15 percent of male senior leaders and 24 percent of female entry-level professionals, according to the findings of a McKinsey/LeanIn.org report, which surveyed 423 organizations and 65,000 employees. The report calls this a "microaggression."[2]

Even after added focus on diversity and racial equity in the workplace, women of color continue to face significant bias and discrimination at work, the researchers found. "While all women are more likely than men to face microaggressions that undermine them professionally—such as being interrupted and having their judgement questioned—women of color often experience these microaggressions at a higher rate," the authors of the report wrote.

Women are still considerably underrepresented at all ranks of management. And on a day-to-day experience at work, "they were more likely than men to have their competence questioned and their authority undermined," according to this analysis. "Women of color and other women with traditionally marginalized identities are especially likely to face disrespectful behavior."

Angela F. Williams, 58, the first Black president and chief executive of United Way Worldwide, leading about 1,100 community United Way operations in more than 40 countries and territories, elaborated on this to me. "When you talk about what are some of the challenges as a leader, as a woman, but especially as the Black woman or Black person, when you show up at the table, even if you're the number one, people still question you, they still challenge your leadership."

She went a little deeper. "And as a Black female leader, we're not trying to break through a glass ceiling. We're trying to break through a concrete ceiling. If you could go back and look at the numbers from the seventies and eighties and fast-forward to now, there has been incremental improvement, but not wholesale improvement. I tell women of color to not be afraid of failure. Don't be afraid of 'no'; no is just a word. Do not attach emotion to that word. When you run into an obstacle that's in front of you, look to your right or left and just walk around. Be comfortable in your skin and be authentic."

That's why I created a separate chapter to address these workplace concerns women face. These concerns ratchet up with age and the amount of time out of the workplace. There are no speedy solutions and, in the years ahead, we must press for more ways to urge companies to address the hiring bias and internal roadblocks that have continued too long. Leadership needs to be held accountable in order for progress to truly take hold, both culturally and within formal business practices.

For now, many women can act to make the workplace more equitable. When the time comes to push ahead in your workplace or get back on board where you left off, those negative feelings you may have internalized must be confronted and pushed aside. There is no wiggle room for believing that you need to look young to succeed.

To start, you might keep "a diary and make a note of what triggers you to compromise yourself or give your power away," Marcus advises the women over 50 she works with.

Women, as they pass 50 in the workplace, need to be tactical and preemptive to resist future pushback and being marginalized. Now that we're showing outward age signs, we need to be more aware of doing things to stay on the playing field and at the top of our game, Marcus said. One of those things is truly knowing what your talents and skills are and what sets you apart.

TAKE CONTROL

I learned from my 22-year-old niece, Shannon, a shrewd way women can take control. She was new to her job, which was remote-only when she was onboarding. During the first week, her manager had scheduled training sessions for new employees that ran for close to three hours a pop.

She found it difficult to absorb all the new information in a way she felt would set her up for future success. So, she called him. Yes, an actual phone call and was direct in explaining her concerns.

He *heard* her and acknowledged her clearly defined, logical, not "woe is me" points and promptly dialed back the sessions to a tighter time frame.

Shannon took control. I wish I had that confidence at her age. Why let yourself be set up for failure, if you can speak out politely and with cogent talking points to support what you need to do your best?

Women, myself included, need to take that chance of being told *no* in order to stay on the job and, frankly, get a job. You can't just accept what is told to you if you have concerns that will impact your work and your career moving forward.

That clear-eyed sense of being direct and forthright that Shannon showed on her first week is my new motivating image when I start to acquiesce when my gut tells me that something's not working for me, and, ultimately, my employer.

Speak Up

Many women are hardwired to want people to like us, to go with the flow. In today's workplace, that habit must get kicked to the curb. Kindness is good, but not standing up for yourself is not.

Support other women your age. Gallup's research found that women tend to be more effective managers and more engaged workers, and that gender-diverse companies are more profitable. That said, a Gallup random sample found that men are twice as likely as women to have a leadership position.[3]

"So, if female managers are already bringing all their talents to bear to exceed expectations and advance, speaking up for other women may feel like special pleading. Speaking up for themselves may endanger their entire careers," the researchers concluded.

So what! Do it! I believe that equipped with the correct negotiating skills, more women will sway their bosses to make them upper-level managers in today's workplace and to negotiate higher pay and better positions before accepting a position. We all know that once you are inside the gates, pay raises are often marginal at best. It's that starting salary that makes all the difference. Never give a salary range that you wouldn't be comfortable accepting if asked in an interview. You can be sure the offer will come in at the low end of your must-have scale.

You'd be foolish to be reticent about negotiating for your own interests. It's true that in my research, I found that women experience repercussions when they negotiate on behalf of themselves. It's OK for women to negotiate assertively on behalf of others. It's the mama bear role of taking care of those who work for us. But when you go at it just as aggressively for yourself, it can backfire.

Get mad. The old iron fist, velvet glove comes to mind. When it's your own promotion or pay at stake, more than ever you need to stay cool and calm on the outside and tough inside. Do not be dismissed. This is a case of nothing ventured, nothing gained. Go for the gain.

But if it's a raise you're after, you will be expected to justify what you're asking for, period. There's no soft shoe here. This is an Irish step dance that must be fast and precise, and have a wee bit of stomp.

It requires a list of why you, why now, why you deserve it. You might begin with hard numbers on what others at your level are earning, followed by the scores you've accomplished for the employer, say, revenues generated. Goals met. It's a sum game in black and white that is measurable. No emotion. Just the facts.

Remember if you don't ask and toot your own horn, your career will stall. Negotiation is not just once a year. It's ongoing. Asking for more money is just one ask in a continual set of moves to keep abreast of the times. Workplaces are shifting constantly as everyone is adjusting to the new shape of things. It's your job to take control and steer your own course. No one will do it for you. Asking is not something that's nice, it's necessary. So, if you are stuck in the "nice girls don't talk about money" world, get over it! Today's workplace will spit you out or ignore you altogether.

One way to get noticed is to ask for those highly visible stretch projects. Men ask for those assignments four times more than we do. To keep your career moving as you charge through the next decade or two, you must constantly demonstrate that you're achievement-oriented. Time is of the essence; this is not a waiting game.

Look for a sponsor, not a mentor. You want to find ways to work with people you know and who would sponsor you if they saw your work close-up. They'll help to develop you because they think you are great and they are not put off by your age. But will push you ahead and suggest you for prominent assignments. As Williams told me, this is particularly important for women of color: "Unless you have an advocate, or someone that's willing to bring you along and introduce you, people of color still don't have that access to many opportunities."

Finally, ask for training that can advance you. It can be awkward to request a spot in a personal development workshop when you reach a certain level in an organization or have been there for a significant number of years, but it can benefit your career. The truth is higher-ups and managers often see that as a sign that you're not slowing down or stepping back. Quite the opposite, you want to keep learning and to discover innovative ways of working for yourself and the organization. That's a message you want to send.

START A BUSINESS

Women over 50 have been starting businesses at a quicker clip than any other cohort globally. Part of that movement is a reaction to a workplace where women aren't valued. Without question. the overwhelming need for work-life balance that the pandemic made painfully real has pushed many women to consider starting their own business. When you're the boss, you can have control.

If you've got a good idea, I encourage you to follow that desire. One thing that's true about being your own boss—age isn't a drawback. If you have a solid, strong business plan as your base, you're on your way.

My research has shown that women are successful entrepreneurs because they go slow—which interestingly is one of the same qualities that makes women outperform men as investors over time. We are deliberate. We think things through. No rash moves.

We do our research and homework ahead of time. We're collaborative. We take baby steps and start in stages. We give a business time to grow. And we tend to stick to our knitting and launch in fields where we have previously worked and have knowledge.

As it is for all older workers, the stories we tell ourselves—that we haven't been doing anything lately and our skills are sadly behind the times, for example—cling to us and can prevent us from starting a business, getting ahead in the workplace, and getting hired. And more than ever, for women, this can be paralyzing.

One of my best friends, a leading photographer, closed her studio shortly after her daughter was born so she could focus on raising her and being the best mom she could. Her husband was rarely home, so she was predominately raising her solo. Now her daughter is in her 20s and her divorce is final.

She's 62 and searching. Yes, she can still take an astounding photograph, has a great eye for composition, and is uber creative, but she says she needs to pay an assistant who can do the digital side of the project and will need to buy all new equipment, which costs thousands of dollars. She's stuck not knowing whether it's worth it to start all over again.

It is, I tell her repeatedly. I believe in her. But she feels outdated. Candidly, I think she's afraid of all the effort it will take to ramp up again and not be dependent on someone else to do half of the job for her. What if she isn't as sharp as she once was?

But mostly it's that inner story reel that she is replaying again and again. And it begins with "Am I too old to learn these new skills? Do I have the energy to do it? Who is going to hire me?"

I know this is a confidence issue and as soon as she gets back into the studio and starts to learn the technology, she will be pulled back into the work she loves and that brings joy to her life and to others. Her network is still strong in that town, and she's a star behind the lens. She just needs to believe in herself and get going again—stop cleaning closets and reorganizing her garden shed.

Like my friend, there's a generation of midlife women in this boat wanting to get back to work. It takes time. My advice for the new workplace is the same as it has been for decades: the best place to start is to understand how all the things you have been doing these past two decades can be repackaged as skills to market to a future employer. If you were caregiving or volunteering, for instance, you were a project manager, a fundraiser, a patient advocate, a bookkeeper, and so on—all transferable skills.

You need to start the conversations with the people around you. Ask people what kind of work they are doing and tell them what you are looking to do. Parents of your children's friends might offer leads or people for you to talk to.

In my friend's case, she attended my mom's funeral, and while talking to my sister-in-law, it came up that my brother and his family were looking for a series of family photos to be taken and asked if she would consider it.

Her answer: Absolutely. They all raved about the pictures. She, of course, was thrilled, and said it was the best day she had had in ages being back at work. But, always humble, she told my brother, "I'm not going to bill you because you are family to me." Luckily, my brother told her she was out of her mind. Business is business and please send a bill. She felt strange about it, but in the end she did.

Although I encouraged her to bill my brother's family (he could afford it), sometimes it's a good strategy to take on a pro bono assignment to recoup your network and have something current to put on your résumé.

In some cases, you need to look at these prospects as passages or building blocks, rather than the occupation you're going to be engaged in for the next decade or more. When you do land a paying gig, chances are, you will work for less income and a lower title than you did before you stepped out, but the key is to get started and be open to new paths as they emerge.

There are things you can do to allay those fears, like taking classes, for example, on GetSetUp (getsetup.io) or LinkedIn to sharpen your tech skills. Make sure you know Microsoft Office basics such as how to work with Microsoft Excel spreadsheets.

A STORY TO INSPIRE

Before we leave this chapter, I can't resist sharing one more amazing story of a woman over 50 who is leading the way in this new world of work—Gayle Jennings-O'Byrne, cofounder of WOCstar Fund (wocstar.com), a venture capital fund that invests in women of color in the technology sector. She took a risk to try something new and go big in the new world of work and she's fearless. I know she will inspire you. She previously worked for JPMorgan as a senior executive in the areas of philanthropy, international government relations, and mergers and acquisitions (M&A).

Her motivation to restart her career in her 50s was spurred by a health crisis. "I was at work in my office at JPMorgan Chase & Company when I got the news that I had cancer, and I thought I can't die in this chair and at this desk without really having made an impact," she recounted to me. "After I got over my fear of dying, I got this courage for living. And at that moment, I became bold and fearless to be a champion for the women I knew, women who looked like me. My journey wasn't the typical one but investing and championing for women is my superpower."

Her advice for women entrepreneurs over 50: "Be a problem-solver. Entrepreneurship is about being a problem-solver. Build things that are big ideas that are going to change how we work and how we live and consume."

Jennings-O'Byrne's 30-year career in technology, investment banking, and M&A training from JPMorgan is what helped her launch her fund. "So much of investing is not solely picking companies and doing the due diligence. It's also helping them build, so we can monetize and return capital to investors," she said.

She utterly owns where she is in her career and how she fits into the new world of work. "I'm now a middle-age Black woman, and I have accomplished a lot in my career. I have made many friendships—both personal and professional—and I am now at an age where I can authentically give that to the startups. I'm at a point in my life where I can take everything I've done and put it toward those that I believe are worthy of investing in. It has become my why."

I asked her what her elevator pitch is: "I'm a Black female capitalist who believes in the markets, who believes in technology, and believes in investing. I invest where the future of technology, products, and services is being built."

And that's precisely the audacious, confident kind of career narrative women over 50 need to weave for themselves to take back their power and move headlong into the new workplace.

Find a Support Group

Joining a networking group of 50+ women like you looking to relaunch is also a good way to navigate your way into the workplace. You can use these get-togethers, often over a meal, to share your fears and dreams, what you used to love most about your work, and what you hated. If the right group is assembled, it becomes a safe place where you can launch your new chapter of work with the support and encouragement of others in the same situation. It's empowering. And you are creating a new power network of strong creative women.

For women starting a business at midlife, this strategy is a good one as well. (As it is for all new entrepreneurs, of course, but for women this can be particularly helpful.) Create a diverse cadre of six to eight women and schedule a regular monthly meeting. Each session should have an agenda of at least two solid things each of you must do monthly to build your business; then discuss how that went and add new ones at the next meetup. This helps to develop the fundamentals of answerability and shoring up, which is crucial in the early days of launching. That's the period when you're second-guessing your decision and feeling isolated and uncertain. To enlist your group, reach out to women you know on the various social media platforms, including Facebook and LinkedIn, but also in your community.

It doesn't just have to be startups. Joining together in general to support one another in the new world of work can be transforming for women at midlife.

Step up, reach out, and ask for help. The workplace as well as how and where we work have been deeply transformed by the digital revolution and the pandemic and will continue to change in the years ahead. These changes can make the work environment seem more overwhelming than ever before and make it difficult to imagine how you can ever get back in the groove.

Turn the switch. Embrace it and look for the shining light of prospects created by these revolutions. This is your time, your new beginning, so turn it around to a positive fresh start with lots of road ahead to get it just right. Find the eye of the hurricane and dance in it, to paraphrase singer/songwriter Brandi Carlile.

Learning Is Fundamental

After retiring from her management position, Marjorie Dorr took art classes, learned to teach yoga, and became a vegan chef. "But I wasn't passionate about what I was doing after feeling part of something bigger than myself and always growing during my career," Dorr told me. "Frankly, I was bored. I felt like I was stuck. I was looking to get back into the flow and trying all kinds of things. I took random classes, but they didn't shift my life."

Then she and her husband moved from New Hampshire to Texas, to see if they might want to retire there. Once there, she applied and was accepted to the nine-month Tower Fellows program offered by the University of Texas at Austin. The program is for adult professionals who are full-time students on campus taking classes across the university.

"It's a great opportunity for adults to learn new skills more relevant for their next chapter, or who just want to go back and take classes that you couldn't take as an undergraduate because you had to be practical," Dorr said. "This is a different chapter to grow in a way that doesn't have the outcome necessarily of making a living."

Rubbing shoulders in the classroom with undergraduates and graduate students "was exhilarating, humbling, frustrating—all of those emotions of a beginner learner," she said. "For me, it felt more frustrating than when I was a 20-year-old. I felt panic at the time. I knew I was creating new neuropathways. My brain had become stale sitting out of the work world for some time."

LEARNING RESOURCES FOR 50+

The Stanford Distinguished Careers Institute (dci.stanford.edu), Harvard's Advanced Leadership Initiative (advancedleadership .harvard.edu), and the University of Notre Dame's Inspired Leadership Initiative (ili.nd.edu), for example, all offer similar educational immersions for people looking for what's next. There is also a program offered by the Halftime Institute (halftimeinstitute.org).

The bottom line is that adult learning is the buzz. People are living longer and working longer. Incessantly boosting professional skills is nonnegotiable to stay on the job, mostly given the rapid-fire speed of technological advancements.

As Bradley Schurman, author of *The Super Age: Decoding Our Demographic Destiny*, always says when we speak together at events such as those presented by Next for Me, "Age @Work: The New Revolution," our sometimes contrarian dialogue about the future of work for the rapidly growing 50+ population: "If you're not *learning*, you're not *earning*."

So true.

Hotel entrepreneur Chip Conley founded the Modern Elder Academy (modernelderacademy.com), in Baja, Mexico, and Santa Fe, New Mexico, dedicated to midlife learning. "For decades, we've learned of the value of lifelong learning, but what's important to and how a person learns at 30 years old is different than when you're 60," Conley, who is also the author of *Wisdom at Work: The Making of a Modern Elder*, explained to me. "This is why we're seeing the emergence of 'long life learning' focused on helping midlifers and beyond live a life that is as deep and meaningful as it is long." (Conley was named a 2019 Next Avenue Influencer in Aging.)

Washington, DC, resident Dr. Lisa K. Fitzpatrick, founder of Grapevine Health, has attended four sessions at the Modern Elder Academy (MEA). "I truly believe we should all be lifelong learners," she said. "I was thinking about how to pivot my career and started exploring what it might be like to become an entrepreneur and on that journey, I learned about MEA. It came at a time when I was really burned out. And needed to be in a different environment."

The basic premise of adult education is metamorphosing. "The lifelong learning concept is happening more and more for people across the arc of their careers because the world is changing, and the skill sets that are necessary are changing," said Thomas Schreier Jr., founding director of the Inspired Leadership Initiative at the University of Notre Dame. "People are finding themselves at a dead end with no idea of where to go.

"Maybe the right idea is that you never really graduate from your university," he added. "The academic world has not been preparing people for a portfolio career. It is going to have to adapt to help people have these multitrack careers."

One of my favorite learning opportunities for those transitioning to work at a nonprofit is the University of Connecticut's Encore!Connecticut (dpp.uconn.edu/encore-connecticut), which assists corporate and public sector professionals, mostly 50+, transitioning to management opportunities in the nonprofit sector. It also offers education in nonprofit leadership, management, operations, and funding strategies and practices. The program helps with nonprofit job-search strategies and résumé restructuring. Students also work on a two-month project with a nonprofit organization.

Many public colleges offer free or reduced tuition for both audited and credit courses for those 50+. AARP provides a list of state-by-state programs. University alumni centers offer live webinars, virtual lectures, and excursions. At Duke University, my alma mater, for example, Lifelong Learning for Alumni is a one-stop resource to link to a smorgasbord of online learning opportunities.

Other options to find classes include adult education centers, local libraries, community colleges, and Osher Lifelong Learning Institutes (osherfoundation.org), One Day University (onedayu .com), a subscription service, offers live streaming lectures and recorded talks. Free or low-priced online classes are available through sites like Coursera (coursera.org), EdX (edx.org), The Great Courses (thegreatcourses.com), LinkedIn Learning, MasterClass (masterclass.com), Skillshare (skillshare.com), TED Talks (ted.com /talks), and Udemy (udemy.com).

The Oasis Institute offers Oasis Everywhere (oasiseverywhere.org), a virtual lifelong learning platform with a menu of online classes for those 50 and older. GetSetUp (getsetup.io/classes) is an interactive, education platform for the 50+ set delivering virtual education to upskill older adults in the use of software and apps, among other subjects.

"Many older adults are coming back to learn how to make extra income from home and how to launch a business," said Neil Dsouza, CEO and founder of GetSetUp. "They aren't looking for a certificate or a degree. It is very practical."

AARP Skills Builder for Work (aarp.org/work/skills-builder) is a suite of free courses including Microsoft Office fundamentals and other learning options.

My hope is that, as the new world of work unfolds, the Department of Labor steps up and reforms the American Job Centers it funds, so that they provide the free help to job seekers over 50. The nearly 2,400 centers are located throughout the United States, but until now have largely ignored the older workforce and its needs.

The tools are there. These centers (CareerOneStop.org) offer help with résumés, interviewing, free training, and coaching. If you haven't done a résumé in 20 years or been on a job interview, you *need* this resource.

The Brookings Economic Studies Program's 2020 report concluded:

> Our proposed reforms would tailor the services offered at the American Jobs Centers to better meet the needs of a workforce that is considerably older on average than in the past. Job centers should include staff who specialize in counseling older clients; they should experiment with job placement programs tailored for their older clients; service staff should provide information and guidance on self-employment options, which are especially attractive to many older workers; and available training programs should include short courses that are customized to older workers' learning needs and styles.[1]

I second that!

To help an aging population continue to work and earn is not only good for the financial security of the workers, but it is a win for the economy. An employed worker pays taxes and buys goods and services. The is something the Department of Labor should strongly support.

"The need for workers to keep pace with fast-moving economic, cultural, and technological changes, combined with longer careers, will add up to great swaths of adults who need to learn more than generations past—and faster than ever," Luke Yoquinto, a research associate at the MIT AgeLab and coauthor of *Grasp: The Science Transforming How We Learn*, told me in an interview for the *New York Times*.

BENEFITS OF LEARNING

By 2034, the number of adults age 65+ will outnumber those under the age of 18, according to the Census Bureau.[2] "That growth of older age demographics will translate to new demand for enrichment in the form of digital education," Yoquinto said. "I would say that, for both good and ill, older demographics are going to serve as a proving ground for learning technologies in the coming years."

And while learning is truly fundamental to both staying on the job and moving to new fields of work, there is something more soulful and enriching about learning at this stage of life. It is the added value that it brings to us that makes our world interesting and lights up our curiosity. That in turn impacts our success at work and in our lives.

The journey to appreciate something we didn't know before or weren't exposed to also builds the resilience necessary to weather setbacks in our lives and our work.

"One of the things that makes us resilient is that when we see a challenge, and when we face a struggle, we engage with it, rather than shut down," Simon Sinek, author of *The Infinite Game* and *Start with Why*, told me. "What I have learned from my career is that something I learned over here helps me over there. Even if I don't know that is happening, any kind of learning benefits all aspects of life."

Sinek, for instance, is a bit of a dance aficionado. "My dancer friends kept telling me I should take classes, and it would help me and my love of the medium. I begrudgingly agreed, and I took some basic ballet classes."

He explained to me that those classes helped his emerging work as a public speaker. "My posture is much better," he said. "I move more effortlessly across the stage from my hips, instead of my shoulders."

Resilience is a word that gets tossed around a lot, I know, but it truly is an essential part of our career and work success. When you're in the process of learning, your viewpoint changes, and you spot connections that you never noticed before.

"Resilience is about being adaptable in a variety of different circumstances," said Dorie Clark, who teaches executive education at Duke University's Fuqua School of Business and is the author of *The Long Game: How to Be a Long-Term Thinker in a Short-Term World.* "It is a combination of being able to pick yourself up when there are setbacks, but also it is about having the kind of cross-training necessary to be flexible in an uncertain world where we don't know what is around the corner."

If you are starting over in a new career or a new job, launching a business right now, or working remotely, you probably are facing all sorts of new challenges and possibly being a greenhorn beginner all over again and not the one who has all the answers.

Face it. This can be mind-blowing psychologically. You will need to step back and look at your situation with some perspective. "People who commit themselves to a life of learning show up with curiosity," Sinek said. "They show up with interest. They show up with a student's mindset. You don't have to be curious about everything. You have to be curious about some things."

Those who habitually and deliberately engage in learning become more self-confident about their ability to figure things out, according to Beverly Jones, my good friend, go-to executive career coach, fellow dog-walker, and author of *Think Like an Entrepreneur, Act Like a CEO* and *Get Your Happy at Work.* "Each time they hit a bump, they spend less time lamenting and quickly turn to determining what they must learn in order to climb out of the hole," she said.

Then too, learners foster a more optimistic outlook. "In part, this is because each time you become aware of learning something new it feels like a victory," Jones said. "You maintain the positivity that is a key to resilience."

No one learns in the same way. "I can't read a book a week," Sinek told me. "I learn by having conversations. I like talking to people who know more than me about any particular subject. I love peppering them with questions. And I love trying to say back in my own words what I think they are telling me to see if I understand it."

For Cuyahoga County prosecutor in Cleveland Gayle Williams-Byers, learning is "that extra oomph to turn off the crazy in life and pour yourself into something that is fantastic that you can benefit from," she said.

I am a perpetual student, so all of this resonates with me. That's why I chose a career and a life as a journalist and writer, so, like Sinek, I could pepper people with questions, people far smarter and more worldly than me. It has made my life richer. It has kept me growing and my world of work alive, ever changing, and challenging.

It can do the same for you.

As the Irish poet William Butler Yeats wrote: "Happiness is neither virtue nor pleasure nor this thing nor that but simply growth. We are happy when we are growing."

Afterword

Thanks for riding along with me and for your trust. My purpose has been to guide you into the new world of work with self-confidence, a touch of bravado, and a desire to dream. As my dad always said when I'd start to feel lost and unsure: "You have to dream to get there."

Then he might add a "Holy Mackerel, Kerry, you've got this" for good measure, and I would crack up.

Yes, I am an upbeat lady, and what I've learned from the Covid-19 pandemic is that things change fast. It's unsettling, and the best way to navigate forward is to see change as an opportunity not an obstacle. You must "stay in the light," as my colleague and author of *The Super Age*, Bradley Schurman advised me one day when I was feeling discouraged.

The bulk of this book was dedicated to the big workplace trends emerging for workers 50+—career transition, remote jobs, and entrepreneurship.

Our workplace is transforming, but it has always been a work in progress. It's just moving faster. Discovering ways to stay relevant, challenged, and on the job *will* be your job.

You might not want to transform your work right this minute, and that's fine. Yet, after reading this book, I hope you clearly realize that you can't be complacent. The workplace and how we do our jobs is ever changing. You must stay engaged.

I don't know how this will play out. It's a fool's errand to speculate about the future—what the new world of work will look like as the pandemic unwinds.

But I do know that there are ways you will succeed in it. The truth is when you ask people what they love most about their jobs, they generally don't say the specific day-to-day details of the work they do. They say it's the people they work with, the mission of their employer, the ability to learn new things.

Focus on what you enjoy about your work and bump it up. Engage more with your coworkers and look for interesting assignments. Don't be afraid to be noticed. Raise your hand and take a chance.

It's easy to lay low if you're nervous about being the next in line to be laid off. You keep your head down and simply do your job. The odds are when you step up to take on a new responsibility, you will nail it. Stepping up shows that you are engaged in your work. Employers love that. And it refreshes you. There's that inescapable blast of adrenaline from being out of your comfort zone. Yes!

I have discovered that when someone says they are unhappy at work and you peel it all back, the real cause is boredom. They feel stuck. The work is repetitive. They feel invisible. They aren't getting promoted anymore.

If this smacks of you, or you are discouraged with a job search, do something. Enroll in a class. When you gain knowledge, you see the world around you differently. As author Bruce Rosenstein writes in *Create Your Future the Peter Drucker Way*, it's your responsibility to "remain relevant" in your work. Rosenstein told me: "Drucker, a management guru, believed that education never ended for a successful knowledge worker."

Clean your office. Hang on. I'm serious. Decluttering is therapeutic. You're saying, "I value this. I don't value that." It's a hands-on way to make decisions about your life.

Post a positive image to inspire you in your office. I call mine "going to my happy place." It calms me down when I focus on that image and my attitude shifts. Try it!

Volunteer. Doing something for someone else always makes you feel better.

Imagine you are an entrepreneur running Me Inc. It's an emboldening turn of the table and realigns your psyche. You approach your work with more ownership and more accountability. You feel more in control.

Explore enjoyment with coworkers or colleagues on nonbusiness activities. This can be a dog-walking group or volunteering or a book club or organized bowling outing once a month.

Finally, and this is my best-loved, favorite piece of advice—laugh! A Gallup poll found that people who smile and laugh at work are more engaged in their jobs (this holds true for life in general, of course). And the more engaged you are, the happier and more enthusiastic you'll be. People will notice. It's infectious, in a good way. You will succeed!

Life is riddled with the unexpected. In the final stages of editing this manuscript, in fact, it happened to me. I was offered a full-time position as a senior columnist and on-air expert at Yahoo Finance. I honestly did not see this one coming. It all happened at lightning speed from the first call with the recruiter to saying yes.

At 61, this new challenge and chapter makes me smile. As my friend and colleague Marci Alboher, Encore.org's vice president and author of *The Encore Career Handbook*, immediately said when I shared my news: "That is such a plum gig for you. In fact, if you manage this properly, I feel like it could be a lifestyle improvement as well, and how about your own story about the power of getting new big roles at this stage of life? Could you be walking the walk any better?"

At 50+ you, too, have the forte and talent to take control of the things you can and the confidence to take a leap for something new when it appears. In that spirit, I wish you joy as you explore and craft new ways to find work that keeps you happy and healthy—the supreme badges of success.

I'm on the road with you!

'Til we meet again, take good care.

Notes

Foreword

1. https://www.transamericainstitute.org/research/workers

Chapter 1

1. https://www.fedsmallbusiness.org/medialibrary/FedSmallBusiness
   /files/2021/45-entrepreneuers-aarp-report
2. https://www.oracle.com/a/ocom/docs/applications/hcm/2020-hcm-ai
   -at-work-study.pdf
3. https://www.bls.gov/news.release/eci.nr0.htm; https://fred.stlouisfed.org
   /series/LNS12024230; https://crr.bc.edu/briefs/how-has-covid-19-affected
   -older-workers-labor-force-participation; https://crr.bc.edu/wp-content
   /uploads/2021/11/IB_21-20.pdf
4. https://www.conference-board.org/blog/labor-markets/2022-salary
   -increase-budgets
5. https://www.wolterskluwer.com/en/news/more-than-half-of-us-states-to
   -institute-a-minimum-wage-increase-in-2022
6. https://globalcoalitiononaging.com/wp-content/uploads/2021/06/
   GCOA_Employers-Role-Covid-19_Winning-in-the-Vastly-Changed-World
   -of-Work_June-2021_FINAL.pdf
7. https://www.microsoft.com/en-us/worklab/work-trend-index/hybrid
   -work
8. https://www.generation.org/wp-content/uploads/2021/07/Meeting-the
   -Worlds-Midcareer-Moment-July-2021.pdf
9. https://www.aarp.org/work/working-at-50-plus/info-2020/employer-age
   -diversity-survey.html
10. https://www.aarp.org/research/topics/economics/info-2021/older-workers
    -new-skills-covid-19-pandemic.html
11. https://www.hiringlab.org/2021/03/16/remote-job-postings-double/

12. https://www.theladders.com/press/data-high-paying-remote-work-oppor
tunities-leap-more-than-1000
13. https://www.nber.org/system/files/working_papers/w24489/w24489.pdf

Chapter 2

1. https://www.shrm.org/foundation/ourwork/initiatives/the-aging-work
force/documents/age-diverse%20workforce%20executive%20briefing.pdf
2. The conference was hosted by the University of Iowa College of Public
Health and nonprofit Transamerica Institute, with funding provided by
NextFifty Initiative.
3. https://www.tcd.ie/news_events/articles/young-and-restless-old-and
-focused-age-differences-in-mind-wandering

Chapter 3

1. https://www.mckinsey.com/featured-insights/future-of-work/the-future
-of-work-after-covid-19
2. https://www.hbs.edu/managing-the-future-of-work/Documents/research
/hiddenworkers09032021.pdf
3. https://www.bls.gov/ooh/healthcare/home.htm
4. https://www.bls.gov/ooh/community-and-social-service/substance
-abuse-behavioral-disorder-and-mental-health-counselors.htm
5. https://www.bls.gov/ooh/community-and-social-service/substance
-abuse-behavioral-disorder-and-mental-health-counselors.htm#tab-8
6. https://www.bls.gov/ooh/computer-and-information-technology/home
.htm
7. https://www.bls.gov/ooh

Chapter 4

1. https://www.sciencedirect.com/science/article/pii/S2352827321001300?via
%3Dihub; https://www.ncbi.nlm.nih.gov/pmc/articles/PMC8255239

Chapter 5

1. https://www.hbs.edu/managing-the-future-of-work/Documents/research
/hiddenworkers09032021.pdf
2. https://www.rosalynncarter.org/wp-content/uploads/2021/09/210140-RCI
-National-Surveys-Executive-Summary-Update-9.22.21.pdf
3. https://www.hbs.edu/managing-the-future-of-work/Documents/research
/hiddenworkers09032021.pdf
4. https://reachire.com/hiring-partners/partner-brand-schneider-electric

Chapter 7

1. https://www.flexjobs.com/blog/post/does-working-remotely-save-you
   -money
2. https://www.microsoft.com/en-us/worklab/work-trend-index/hybrid
   -work
3. https://crr.bc.edu/wp-content/uploads/2020/06/IB_20-9.pdf
4. https://www.flexjobs.com/blog/post/benefits-of-remote-work

Chapter 8

1. https://www.generation.org/wp-content/uploads/2021/07/Meeting-the
   -Worlds-Midcareer-Moment-July-2021.pdf

Chapter 9

1. https://www.bc.edu/content/dam/files/research_sites/agingandwork/pdf
   /publications/FS40-Trendsinself-employment.pdf
2. https://www.kellogg.northwestern.edu/faculty/jones-ben/htm/Age%20
   and%20High%20Growth%20Entrepreneurship.pdf
3. https://www.score.org/resource/wheres-money-10-types-small-business
   -financing-and-how-qualify
4. https://www.sba.gov/sba-learning-platform/boots-business#section
   -header-0

Chapter 10

1. https://www.gallup.com/workplace/352529/wellbeing-stats-women
   -workplace-show-need-change.aspx
2. https://www.mckinsey.com/featured-insights/diversity-and-inclusion
   /women-in-the-workplace
3. https://www.gallup.com/workplace/352529/wellbeing-stats-women
   -workplace-show-need-change.aspx

Chapter 11

1. https://www.brookings.edu/wp-content/uploads/2020/11/ES-11.19.20
   -Abraham-Houseman.pdf
2. https://www.census.gov/library/stories/2019/12/by-2030-all-baby-boomers
   -will-be-age-65-or-older.html

Additional Resources

CHAPTER 1: THE NEW WORLD OF WORK

aarp.org

generation.org

Indeed.com

theladders.com

workplaceintelligence.com

CHAPTER 2: WHY OLDER WORKERS ROCK

coachingfederation.org

lifeplanningnetwork.org

retirementcoachesassociation.org

CHAPTER 3: WHERE THE JOBS ARE AND WHERE THEY'LL BE

Department of Labor's CareerOneStop: careeronestop.org

O*NET® Career Exploration Tools: onetcenter.org/tools.html

The Occupational Outlook Handbook: bls.gov/ooh/

CHAPTER 4: TAKING CONTROL OF YOUR FUTURE

Clifton Strengths assessment: gallup.com/cliftonstrengths
/en/252137/home.aspx

Myers-Briggs Personality Test: mbtionline.com

The Certified Financial Planner Board of Standards: CFP.net

The Financial Planning Association: onefpa.org

The National Association of Personal Financial Advisors: napfa.org

CHAPTER 5: JOB-HUNTING STRATEGIES

AARP Resume Advisor: aarp.org/work/resume-advisor

AARP Skills Builder for Work: aarp.org/workskills

AvidCareerist: avidcareerist.com

Career Directors International: careerdirectors.com

Career Trend: careertrend.net

Chameleon Resumes: chameleonresumes.com

Executive Career Brand: executivecareerbrand.com

grammarly.com

Great Resumes Fast: greatresumesfast.com

irelaunch.com

jobscan.com

LinkedIn resume writer contacts: linkedin.com/services
/l2/resume-writers

National Résumé Writers Association: thenrwa.com

NextAvenue.org

OnRamp Fellowship: onrampfellowship.com

Path Forward: pathforward.org

Schneider Electric's Return-to-Work program: reachire.com/hiring
-partners/partner-brand-schneider-electric

vmock.com

Web designer sites: fiverr.com; linkedin.com/services; upwork.com; taskrabbit.com

Web hosting sites: dreamhost.com; fatcow.com; godaddy.com; hostinger.com; hostwinds.com; and wix.com

WorkingNation: workingnation.com

CHAPTER 6: SHOWTIME

AARP Employer Pledge Program: aarp.org/work/job-search /employer-pledge-companies/

aarp.org/volunteer/

bridgespan.org

encorebostonnetwork.org

glassdoor.com

idealist.org

payscale.com

retirementjobs.com

salary.com

Second Act Stories Podcast: secondactstories.org

Toastmasters Club: toastmasters.org

volunteermatch.org

CHAPTER 7: REMOTE WORK

AARP's job board: jobs.aarp.org

careerbuilder.com

coursera.org

fiverr.com

flexjobs.com

flexprofessionalsllc.com

freelancer.com

getsetup.io

glassdoor.com

GLG: glginsights.com

happify.com

headspace.com

indeed.com

jobspresso.co

linkedin.com/learning

LinkedIn Jobs: linkedin.com/jobs

monster.com

National Telecommuting Institute: ntiathome.org

nytimes.com/wirecutter/office/home-office

ratracerebellion.com

remote.co

sidehusl.com

skipthedrive.com

The Acceleration Project (TAP): theaccelerationproject.org

toptal.com

udemy.com

upwork.com

virtualvocations.com.

weworkremotely.com

Work At Home Vintage Experts: wahve.com

Working Nomads: workingnomads.co/jobs

ziprecruiter.com

CHAPTER 8: CAREER TRANSITION

authentic happiness questionnaires: authentichappiness.sas
   .upenn.edu/testcenter

encore.org

generation.org

CHAPTER 9: BE YOUR OWN BOSS

aarp.org/work/small-business

Boots to Business: sbavets.force.com/s/b2b-course-information

edx.org

eiexchange.com

experieneurship.com/programs/experience-incubator

flexjobs.com

flexprofessionalsllc.com

freelancer.com

gofundme.com

ifundwomen.com

indiegogo.com

kickstarter.com

republic.com

sba.gov

score.org

taskrabbit.com

upwork.com

usa.gov/business

virtualvocations.com

weworkremotely.com

Work At Home Vintage Experts: wahve.com

workforyourself.aarpfoundation.org

CHAPTER 10: CAREER ADVANCEMENT FOR WOMEN OVER 50

bonniemarcusleadership.com

irelaunch.com

nextavenue.org/2021-influencers-in-aging

reachire.com

secondactwomen.com

wocstar.com

CHAPTER 11: LEARNING IS FUNDAMENTAL

advancedleadership.harvard.edu

coursera.org

dci.stanford.edu

dpp.uconn.edu/encore-connecticut

edx.org

getsetup.io

halftimeinstitute.org

ili.nd.edu

masterclass.com

modernelderacademy.com

oasiseverywhere.org

onedayu.com

osherfoundation.org

skillshare.com

ted.com/talks

thegreatcourses.com

udemy.com

umac.umn.edu

BOOKS

Boomer Reinvention: How to Create Your Dream Career Over 50
    by John Tarnoff

Create Your Future the Peter Drucker Way by Bruce Rosenstein

Embrace the Work, Love Your Career and *The Myth of the Nice Girl:
    Achieving a Career You Love Without Becoming a Person You
    Hate* by Fran Hauser

The Encore Career Handbook by Marci Alboher

55, Underemployed, and Faking Normal: Your Guide to a Better Life
    by Elizabeth White

*Find Your Happy at Work: 50 Ways to Get Unstuck, Move Past
    Boredom, and Discover Fulfillment* and *Think Like an
    Entrepreneur, Act Like a CEO* by Beverly Jones

From Start-Up to Grown-Up by Alisa Cohn

Grasp: The Science Transforming How We Learn
    by Luke Yoquinto

*How to Live Forever: The Enduring Power of Connecting the
Generations* by Marc Freedman

Leapfrog: The New Revolution for Women Entrepreneurs by Nathalie
Molina Niño

*The Long Game: How to Be a Long-Term Thinker in a Short-Term
World* by Dorie Clark

The New Retirement: The Ultimate Guide to the Rest of Your Life
by Jan Cullinane

*Not Done Yet! How Women Over 50 Regain Their Confidence and
Claim Workplace Power* by Bonnie Marcus

Purpose and a Paycheck and *UnRetirement* by Chris Farrell

Second-Act Careers by Nancy Collamer

Start with Why? and *The Infinite Game* by Simon Sinek

The Super Age: Decoding Our Demographic Destiny by Bradley
Schurman

Wisdom at Work: The Making of a Modern Elder by Chip Conley

Index

About the Author

Kerry Hannon is a workplace futurist and a leading strategist on career management, entrepreneurship, personal finance, and retirement. She is a frequent TV, podcast, and radio commentator and is a sought-after keynote speaker at conferences. Kerry is the bestselling and award-winning author of 14 books, including *Great Pajama Jobs: Your Complete Guide to Working from Home* and *Never Too Old to Get Rich: The Entrepreneur's Guide to Starting a Business Mid-Life*, a number one bestseller on Amazon and selected by the *Washington Post* for its Book-of-the-Month Club.

Other bestselling and award-winning books penned by Kerry include *Money Confidence: Really Smart Financial Moves for Newly Single Women, Great Jobs for Everyone 50+: Finding Work That Keeps You Happy and Healthy . . . and Pays the Bills, Love Your Job: The New Rules for Career Happiness, Getting the Job You Want After 50*, and *What's Next? Finding Your Passion and Your Dream Job in Your Forties, Fifties, and Beyond*.

Kerry is currently a senior columnist and on-air expert at Yahoo! Finance. She was previously an expert columnist, opinion writer, and regular contributor to the *New York Times, MarketWatch*, and *Forbes*, and was the PBS website NextAvenue.org personal finance and entrepreneur expert. She has also worked as a writer, columnist, and editor for *USA Today, U.S. News & World Report*, and *Money* magazine and as a contributor to the *Wall Street Journal*.

Kerry lives in Washington, DC, and Boston, Virginia, with her husband, documentary producer and editor Cliff Hackel, and her Labrador retriever, Elmore "Elly." Follow Kerry on Twitter @KerryHannon, visit her website at KerryHannon.com, and check out her LinkedIn profile at linkedin.com/in/kerryhannon.